For The Life Of Me

To our dear parents
Basil and Lilian Burton

For The Life Of Me

Gerald D. Burton

With additional material by
Angela E. Harris

First published in Great Britain in 2016
by
Angela E. Harris
a.e.harris@mypostoffice.co.uk

Copyright © 2016 Angela E. Harris

ISBN 978-0-9955639-0-2

Typesetting by
ReesPrint
1 Little Howe Close
Radley, Abingdon
Oxon OX14 3AJ
reesprint@gmail.com

Print Production by
St Andrews Press of Wells
St Andrews Park
Princes Road, Wells,
Somerset BA5 1TE
www.standrewspress.co.uk

Contents

Foreword   vii

1   **Bene Qui Latuit**   1

Before my time   1

My childhood   4

Life at the shops   11

More of life at the shops   19

Life's tapestry   22

Reflections on some Hullisms   25

Holidays   26

Hymers College, Hull   29

Six generations of the Harrisons   34

John and Molly Keenan   36

The Caleys   36

2   **Moving On**   41

Living the life   41

Printing as a hobby and a business: 'Types and shadows'...   53

Wells, Somerset   58

A way with words   70

3   **When Words Leave Off**   79

Early musical days   79

Choirs and more   81

The St Hugh Singers   88

Adventures in organ playing   90

Going solo   95

Two of Gerald's singing teachers   98

'Through all the changing scenes'...   98

A Parting Thought   101

Foreword

The material in this book was intended to be part of the family trees which my brother Gerald spent many years researching. It was not obvious to which set of trees it belonged, but the solution came from Tim Wood, the friendly printer in Wells who knew Gerald. Tim persuaded me that Gerald's relations and many friends would appreciate a separate volume; and so it became a book in its own right.

I came into the world less than 17 months after Gerald, and we shared many aspects of our childhoods. We remained great friends, and often reminisced about our early lives. Our post-war childhoods influenced us greatly, but we were thankfully unaware of the struggles our parents must have had, especially in Hull, which was badly damaged in the Second World War. Times were not easy for them, with few educational opportunities. Dad had been injured as a young soldier in the First World War, and our mother had had to help out at home and in her father's shop. They worked hard to support us, and our education was a priority. We benefited greatly from their many skills, their wisdom, sociability and their generosity of spirit.

Gerald had an accomplished life in his chosen fields. He loved detail, and whatever he did, he achieved to a high level. After his death from cancer in 2008, I discovered a treasure trove of cherished letters, articles, photographs, concert programmes and music reviews, as well as his vast book collection. I found copies of letters to and from his friends, and his letters to our parents, which he had reclaimed. His forthright opinions about today's use of English emerged, and I am certain he intended to publish these in some form.

Gerald had already written some of his memoirs, and these have been reproduced here. I am convinced too, that he had planned to use his personal archive to write further episodes of his life. I am grateful for the days of real letters, either typed or carefully handwritten in his stylish script. I perused his archive with great interest, and chose some golden nuggets of personal history to supplement his musings. Gerald was a special person to his relations and many friends, and my wish is that they find pleasure in reading about the Gerald they knew, and that his tales raise a smile or two. Personal memories of Gerald may be triggered along the way.

I found that Dr Robin Rees, a long-standing friend of Gerald, was willing to edit and typeset Gerald's books. Without Robin's invaluable help, I doubt I would have completed the project. He has been a constant source of encouragement and his attention to detail has been indispensable at every stage.

The saying, 'A picture is worth a thousand words' may not be entirely accurate. I am nonetheless most grateful to all those who have kindly provided pictures on these pages: John Allen, 100; Fiona Care, 101; Bill Craig, 93; Hull History Centre, 12; Margaret and Les Hunt, 59; Hymers College, Hull, 30, 31, 33; Mendip Voices, 68, 69; Eric Purchase Photography, 58, 60; Keith Saunders Photography, 64; Mike Shore, 70; and Strode Opera, 99. I would also like to thank Sam Featherstone for scanning most of the illustrations, and transferring them to compact disc for insertion into the book.

This volume is a record of Gerald's enthusiasm for life, his lively wit, his individuality, and of his extraordinary, ordinary life. My part in this project is my personal tribute to a very dear brother.

Angela Harris
May 2016

1

Bene Qui Latuit

Bene qui latuit bene vixit.
He who has lived in obscurity has lived well.

Ovid

I can't remember for the life of me most of what has happened in my life (not that I've ever taken drugs, though I may have had the odd drink too many sometimes). Many of the winnowings of memory, however, are set down in these pages.

Before my time

My mother was born Lilian Barnes, in Hull on 1 February 1908. She was one of six children, in order: Eva, Lilian, Frank, Catherine, Henry and Laura. Though only the second of them, she always felt that she had been an unwanted child. This must have helped to determine her character for the whole of her life, though it was something she only talked about in her last few years. As evidence that she was unwanted, she related how when, as a baby she was being taken by her mother to be baptised at St Andrew's Church,[1] her mother exclaimed that she had forgotten what she was going to call her. Then she suddenly said, 'Oh, yes, I decided I'd call her after myself'—and so she did. This could explain why Lilian had only one Christian name while her brothers and sisters had two. Certainly Eva did (her middle name was Love, probably after an ancestor whom I have been unable to trace), and so did Henry (Wills, a Devon ancestor). Most if not all of her brothers and sisters were also baptised at St Andrew's—certainly Henry was—and her parents were married there.

My mother was put upon as the drudge of the household at Buckingham Street, in particular doing much to look after her younger brothers and sisters. Conversely, her mother seemed to be unwell or perhaps depressed, and was used to sitting back and letting the children do the chores. Mother attended Buckingham Street School—'Mucky Bucky' was the jibe that pupils of that school had to put up with! Once her mother sent her to buy some dinner plates. At the hardware shop on Holderness Road were piles of plates of various sizes. Mother did her best to remember how big dinner plates were, and bought some that looked the right size: they turned out to be far bigger than required and had to be

---

[1] On the corner of Abbey Street, Holderness Road.

exchanged. There was money to send Eva to high school in those days when one had to pay; not so for my mother.

My mother attended Sunday School at the Brunswick Institute, Durham Street. She recalled that a teacher there, Mrs Hindle, once told her, 'I used to teach your mother'. Mrs Hindle kept a shop selling hats at the top of Durham Street, and her husband had an aerated waters business; later they had a small business in Hornsea.

Of her father's off-licence at Buckingham Street, my mother said there was a lot of money about during the First World War. Especially at the end of the war, when people were celebrating having got through it and getting home, at opening time people would be queuing up for beer. In those days, off-licences sold beer not only in bottles but also on draught, measuring it into customers' jugs. One of the tricks of the trade that Mother once mentioned involved having an inch of cheap beer in the bottom of the measure used for a better beer. On one occasion at that time, a delivery of Crown Stout, cheaper than Guinness, was delivered with a lot of the labels coming off; it was sold as Guinness.

My father Basil Clapham Burton was born in Hull on 14 June 1899. Some 90 years later, I noticed on the Wells Cathedral service list that this was St Basil's Day, supporting my theory that there were Catholic leanings on the Clapham side of the family. My father's mother was Sarah Porritt Burton (née Clapham), from the West Riding hamlet of Fieldhead. She married widower Albert Burton from Louth, Lincolnshire. They had two sons: my father, and his younger brother Leslie, who died at the age of seven. Albert left the family home (we think he was a drunkard), so my father was brought up mainly by Sarah. Father's childhood, including schooling, was split between Scarborough where his grandfather Clapham had retired, and Hull where his mother kept a boarding house. The Scarborough home was run as a boarding house by my father's twin maiden aunts, my father and Sarah helping out in the summer months. He retained a fondness for the town.

During service in the East Yorkshire Regiment in the First World War, my father was shot in the arm and hand, and spent some months in hospitals in Lincoln and Leeds. He always found employment, but regretted that his injuries prevented him from becoming a policeman.

My mother was my father's second wife. His first, Olive Jessney, died of tuberculosis in 1928, leaving my half-brother Geoffrey, born in 1925. He was brought up by my father and two grandmothers, and for a short time by my mother. When my parents made trips to the seaside before they married, Geoffrey went with them as well as my mother's youngest sister, Laura. Geoffrey was evacuated to Whitby with his secondary school during the Second World War, and when old enough to be called up, was posted to Scotland with the Navy. Post-war he trained as an engineer and was in the Merchant Navy for a few years before taking a shore job. He married Pamela Richardson, and they had two sons: Matthew and Oliver.

The wedding of Lilian Barnes to Basil Burton, 1936

My parents were married at St Mary's Church, Lowgate, Hull, on Sunday morning, 21 June 1936, by the Revd Maurice Clack, a fine priest for whom my mother had a high regard. My mother and he exchanged Christmas letters and cards right up until her death, and Maurice Clack himself, outliving his wife, died in South Africa late in 1987, having worked there for many years.[1]

---

[1] Gerald's sister Angela (AEH) continued the correspondence in the 1980s.

My childhood

In around 1985 I learnt that the Townend Maternity Home, Cottingham Road, Hull, was to be closed. 'At last', I thought, 'some 40 years after my birth, they have finally worked out where all the bad eggs are coming from!' I was born there on 17 June 1944; there too my brother first saw the light of day before me, and my sister after me. Actually, I didn't see the light of day at first, as I was born, highly inconveniently, at half past one in the morning. My father had had his 45th birthday three days beforehand; my mother was 36.

Gerald aged 1, and brother Roger (L)

Kenneth Roger—the name Kenneth was never used—was born on 20 February 1939, and Angela Elizabeth on 2 November 1945. It was decided she should be called Angela Elisabeth—with an 's'—but in the excitement of the moment, my father forgot this instruction and registered her as Angela Elizabeth. For many years, Angela thought her second name was spelt with the 's', as it was on her christening certificate but not on her birth certificate, as she discovered years later.

At Angela's wedding reception, Uncle Henry told a story which I do not remember hearing before, though it turned out that Angela was familiar with it (*too* familiar, I remember from her reaction to the retelling). Apparently years ago local elections were held as near as possible to 1 November. On that date in 1945, my father had phoned for a taxi to take my mother to the maternity home. There was a knock at the front door, and she answered. It was a Labour Party canvasser who asked: 'Are you for Labour?', 'I don't know about *for* Labour', my mother replied, 'but I'm *in* labour!'. Angela was born the next day.

Gerald with Helen Burke of the BBC at a cookery demonstration,
Cottingham, near Hull, 1946

Mother's favourite records that were played on the radio in those days included *We're a couple of swells*, *The trolley song*[1] and *Hungarian Dance No. 5* by Brahms. It may have been one of these that she requested on the extremely popular radio programme *Housewives' Choice* in around 1950. To her disappointment, the record was played when she was out, or at any rate not listening, and the first she knew was when a Mrs Riley from down the street congratulated her!

Energy and fuel were far more expensive, relatively speaking, than they are now. Lights were always turned off when not in use. Even in winter, the only source of heating in the house (apart, of course, from my mother's cooking in the 'scullery'—we didn't call it the kitchen) was the open fire in the middle room. With the passage of time, a lot of coal dust tends to accumulate at the bottom of a coal house, and on one occasion my father bought some cement to make the dust into briquettes. He must

---

[1] Sung respectively by Judy Garland and Fred Astaire in the film *Easter Parade*, and by Judy Garland in *Meet me in St Louis*.

have made the mould or moulds himself, and this piece of ingenuity worked very well. I'm too young to remember the severe winter of early 1947, though Roger remembers snow in great depth. My father's job at that time was collecting milk in churns from farms. Then, and no doubt in other periods of snow, milk churns were pulled on sledges to my father's lorry if he could not even get to the farm gates. One source of fuel for the fire was 'cinders', the spent coke from the gas works on Clough Road. People used to take them home in prams, though whether you had to pay for them I do not know. Father had an advantage there, as of course he had the milk lorry for transport. We knew that prudence had temporarily been thrown to the winds if a fire was lit in the front room; I can only remember that happening at Christmas, but a cheerful, generously stoked and blazing fire was *de rigeur* on the visits of one or another aunt and uncle and cousins.

Gerald aged 2, East Park, Hull,
with his mother watching Angela in the pram

To cope with a shortage of schoolteachers after the war, the government provided accelerated training courses for returning servicemen. Uncle Henry (my mother's brother) took advantage of this—he had been an electrician before the war—and his first teaching job was at Skirlaugh, a village east of Hull. Sometimes, Roger tells me, he solved the problem of getting to school from his home in Summergangs Road by taking a lift on my father's milk lorry. Henry must have had to get up very early to make the rendezvous at the junction of Summergangs Road and Holderness Road, but soon gained his independence by purchasing a BSA Bantam motorbike. Prompted by his example, my father soon bought, for £75, a similar machine. The only difference between the two that I recall was that Henry's had an old-fashioned bulb horn, while my father's sported an electric one.

Like millions of other men in those days, my father religiously posted his football pools coupon every week, and according to Roger it was a win of £90 in 1949 that enabled him to buy the motorbike. The BSA Bantam was a two-stroke, 125-cc machine. To each tankful of petrol you added a quantity of oil, for which the petrol cap served as the measure. My father took me to many places on this machine, though I am able now to recall only one or two experiences. One of these was a motorcycle time trial. All the clocks en route were covered up or stopped somehow, and participants were not allowed to wear watches. As far as I recollect, by guesswork you had to be at a series of checkpoints as closely as possible to the target times. I have a vague idea that when my father was later notified of his result, he had by no means covered himself in glory. I can't have been more than eight as I'm sure we were still living at our first home, in Hardy Street. I haven't a clue what the route was, and somehow we seemed to have chosen the worst weather of the year: cold (my impression is that it was November), with lots of hail; how it stung my cheeks! My mother had made a pair of leggings out of chestnut-coloured material (I can still picture the exact shade), with elasticated waist and hems, but they were no match for the conditions. Never was the warmth of a fire so welcome as on our return.

However, my father was a careful rider: there was just one incident, on a curving road down towards the sea at Filey if I am not mistaken, when the machine skidded on a patch of oil and went sideways for a few yards. I held on grimly to the bike and my father simultaneously, and, though shaken, we were unscathed with just a minor tear in the leggings to show for it. Also we once had a frustrating mile or so along Hedon Road, when the bike wouldn't go faster than about 20 miles an hour because of water in the petrol. After the bike had given years of faithful service, my father braked violently in Ferensway when a woman wandered onto a zebra crossing. The gearbox jammed and the bike never went under its own power again, languishing in the back yard at our next home in Strickland Street for far too long, until somebody paid my father 10 shillings and took it away.

Not surprisingly, in view of the dressmaking jobs she had before she married, my mother was a highly skilled needlewoman. She sewed and knitted all her life: socks were darned, pillow-cases mended, and shirt-collars turned. She could make dresses from patterns too: many was the time, I remember, when she and my sister Angela, in the early 1960s, would argue vehemently about how to interpret some pattern whose paper sections were covering the dining table or, in the case of more ambitious garments, the floor. But these sessions were a firm foundation for my sister's excellent needlework skills. Mother also made many embroidered items. From the early 1950s onwards, she attended embroidery classes at the Hull Regional College of Art in Carr Lane, under the tutelage of Jennifer Gray. Though Mother had formerly done only conventional embroidery, the classes concerned machine- and hand-embroidery techniques. I still have a machine-embroidered table cloth and a framed picture of a horse, worked by my mother. However, the climax of these years of steady activity—one evening a week—was the creation by the evening class and full-time students of embroidered panels depicting events in the life of St John of Beverley, on display in Beverley Minster to this day. Some members of the class did two panels; others, including my mother, did one; each panel bears the name of the executant.[1] The members of the class became firm friends: once in a while there was a 'do' at the house of one of them, at which card games were played, and sandwiches, cakes, tea and sherry served. Names I remember are Gladys Herbert, May Richardson, who never married and was related to the people who started Hornsea Pottery, and the somewhat formal Phyllis Partington, whose father had been a butcher.

Another activity that these ladies shared was membership of the 'Lit. and Phil.', that is to say the Hull Literary and Philosophical Society. In those days, the society's meetings were held in Hammond's restaurant in Ferensway. One evening, my mother returned home to Strickland Street, at once scandalised, embarrassed and amused. The speaker that evening had been the famous naturalist George Cansdale, who had brought some snakes with him. Mother and her embroideress friends, including Phyllis, had good seats near the front. The appearance of a snake sent Phyllis into hysterics, and she could not leave the hall fast enough. Mother told us that Phyllis had drawers and drawers full to the brim with exquisite embroidery and hand knitting. Mother wondered where it all went on her death.

---

[1] The accompanying key in the Minster has my mother's Christian name misspelt as 'Lillian'.

In, if I remember rightly, the 1950s and '60s, my mother had her hair done by a Mr Pyzer at his shop on Carr Lane under the City Hall. Mr Pyzer had a false leg. His assistant was a Miss Harris. The business was in fact called *Maison de Paris*, but Hull women used to phone and ask, 'Is that Mason's?' When Mr Pyzer retired, my mother took her custom to Sylvia Gray.

My father was a lorry driver before running two off-licence shops consecutively for 18 years, followed by retirement at nearly 70. He learnt to drive years before driving tests were introduced in 1935. Before the Second World War, he delivered lemonade to shops in Hull, working for a firm called Straker & Co., run by Ernie Straker. At around the beginning of the war he went to work for PCS Dairies, Southcoates Lane, Hull; you drove in through a gap in a parade of shops, as I recall. At first his job was to collect milk (in churns, as there were no tankers then) from farms in Holderness. During the Blitz, he would negotiate his way back into Hull along roads across which fire hoses snaked, as firefighters fought the massive conflagrations in East Hull. He was the one who would then volunteer to return to the scenes of these fires to serve the firemen with tea and refreshments during the night hours. Father usually referred to his vehicle not as a truck, nor as a lorry, but as a 'rulley', which the dictionary defines as a 'flat four-wheeled dray; lorry'. Roger told me that another employee of PCS Dairies didn't like Father and used to loosen the nuts on the wheels of his lorry. On one occasion Father was driving eastwards across Drypool Bridge, when a wheel came off and trundled into a garage. Father stopped the lorry—which in any case was down on its axle—and retrieved the wheel.

My mother's parents, Frank and Lilian Barnes, kept an off-licence shop at 69 Buckingham Street, Holderness Road, Hull; it was one of the calls on my father's lemonade round, so that is how my parents met. He also earned extra money as a commissionaire at the Metropole Ballroom in West Street, which was blitzed during the war, on a site later occupied by Woolworths.[1] For legal reasons, he was designated 'assistant manager'— somebody had to be in charge!

My father liked to make day excursions. In the 1930s, he once took my half-brother Geoffrey to the National Dance Band Championships in Blackpool, when Len Ibsen and his well-known Hull band had reached the finals. Sometimes Geoffrey would go with Father on his lemonade

---

[1] A family story tells that Dad once met Sir Henry Wood. Best known for his association with London's Promenade Concerts, Sir Henry liked to support provincial orchestras. In 1923 he accepted the conductorship of the amateur Hull Philharmonic Orchestra, travelling three times a year until 1939 to rehearse and conduct its concerts. One of Dad's duties was to take tea to the principals in the break. However, on one occasion a few people were missing. Sir Henry asked Dad to sit down and partake of one of the spare cups of tea, and he asked Dad about his work. *AEH*

rounds. My father also liked variety shows, and in 1962 he obtained tickets for the last performance of the Crazy Gang at the Victoria Palace Theatre in London. Angela recalls when Father hired a box at the Palace Theatre in Hull for the *Billy Cotton Band Show*, and they were pelted with cotton wool balls at the end.

For £305 Father bought on a mortgage a house at 94 Hardy Street, off Cottingham Road, a long street of small terrace houses, gloomy and poky to today's eyes, built in about 1910. He bought it at the time of the marriage in 1936, but his aunt Mary Ann Swain Clapham did not die until 30 April 1937, and under her will he inherited £234.

Hardy Street, Cottingham Road, 1950

When I was a small boy living at Hardy Street, my father was still working for PCS, but he had switched to delivering the milk from the dairy to shops in East Hull. During the school holidays, I would sometimes go with him in the cab, and that is how I came to know the dairy. It was all, no doubt, laughably small-scale by today's standards. On one side was an oily roller conveyor, down which all the dirty bottles went on their way to be washed. In another part was the menacing boiler (the hot metal wall of which you could just squeeze past) that produced the heat for the sterilising system. (In Hull in those days, bottled milk was sterilised rather than pasteurised; the system PCS had was such that each bottle had a skin on the top, which as a child I avoided getting into my mouth at all costs! Sterilising the milk also gave it a slightly off-white colour. But it all depends what you're used to, and at that time pasteurised milk tasted quite disagreeable to me.) The bottles had stoppers with rubber seals, wired to the body of the bottle, and you opened the bottle by pressing the stopper laterally with your thumbs. Later, crown corks were introduced—a great novelty. At school the (free) milk was pasteurised, in $1/_3$-pint bottles with cardboard tops.

There was, in fact, a dairy that delivered door-to-door in Hardy Street. A lady came round with a van, I seem to recall. You put your jug outside the front door with a saucer on top to keep out the dust, and the milk lady filled it—a pint, say—using a measure which she dipped into a big metal can that was replenished from the van.

I often think nowadays that the standard of living at that time, the late 1940s, was roughly the same as one would find today in the Czech Republic and Poland, both of which I have visited in recent years.

The five of us lived at Hardy Street until June 1952, when I was eight. During that time Geoffrey would stay sometimes—presumably when he was not at sea—and he told me that he used to put beer bottles in place of milk bottles in the doorway of a strict Methodist family who lived opposite us there! One day, he brought home a little black mongrel puppy, Suki, which of course we children liked, though my mother, I am sure, thought it a great nuisance. It had not been vaccinated, so not a great deal of time elapsed before it caught distemper and had to be put down. Angela thinks Geoffrey found the dog on the docks, though he thinks he bought it from a man in a pub, and I suppose he would know![1]

Life at the shops

We moved from Hardy Street after my father developed back trouble, which put an end to his job at PCS. In those days, milk crates were made of steel and were not the conveniently light plastic objects of today; even the bottles weighed more than the products of today's glass technology. Moreover, the crates had to be lifted from the back of the lorry onto the barrow or vice versa; tail-lifts and fork-lift trucks lay in the future. Not surprisingly, when he was 52, his back turned out to be no longer up to the job. He was out of work for about six months, and lived on his

---

[1] I recall taking the dog to be 'put down', and riding in the pushchair in the rain, with the dog licking me goodbye. *AEH*

savings because he was too proud to draw the dole. There were abortive plans to take a grocery shop in Scarborough, which had all of us three children highly excited at the prospect of living at the seaside. The reality was more prosaic: we moved to a tiny off-licence of which my father took the tenancy at 4 Strickland Street, which was probably the most run-down street of a large slum area on Hessle Road. All the same, we three children, knowing little of the harsh reality that preoccupied grown-ups, could hardly wait to live behind and over a shop. Over the time of the move itself, my sister and I stayed for a couple of days at our grandma's, 56 East Park Avenue, so as to be out of the way. The Strickland Street property was taken over from a couple called Holmes; I remember the name from my father's exploratory visits, as he had taken me with him on the pillion of his trusty BSA Bantam 125-cc motorbike. The Holmeses must have been a slovenly couple, as an eye-catching feature of the new house was the trails of white insecticide that my parents had scattered all along the skirting boards in the downstairs living room.

The off-licence shop at 4 Strickland Street, Hull

It was the archetypal corner shop and 'beer off', or off-licence. The range of goods kept in those few square feet of floor space was phenomenal. These included: biscuits (weighed out loose from the tins), sweets (from jars; the count lines at a halfpenny and a penny were mostly displayed in the window which gave onto the street), chocolate, beers, stouts and lemonades (on shelves in the other window which gave onto Thorne Terrace; the curved double shop doors were on the corner of the terrace and the street), vegetables (potatoes, onions, carrots, cabbages), cigarettes and tobacco, ice-cream and (latterly) ice lollies, firewood and firelighters, bandages, combs, cakes, bread, milk, and all basic groceries. Sugar my father bought a hundredweight at a time, weighing it out himself on quiet afternoons into dark blue bags of half a pound and a pound—it was cheaper than buying it prepacked. Butter too he bought perhaps seven pounds at a time, to be weighed out into greaseproof paper and carefully wrapped. Then there were the patent medicines, such as Bile Beans, Beecham's Pills and Beecham's Powders, Seidlitz powders, Aspros, somebody's Back and Kidney Pills, and Gunnee's powders. I may not have spelt this last name correctly and have a feeling these may have been a local product. But for all its novelty for us children, my mother must have found the change of circumstances vastly disappointing and depressing, an ever-present reminder of the years of drudgery at Buckingham Street that she thought she had left behind years earlier when she married my father.

Because space was at a premium, it annoyed my father that people brought back empty bottles which they had not bought in our shop. Perhaps people needed coppers for the electricity meter in the evening when the grocery shops on the main road were closed. My father soon solved the problem as regards the lemonade and beer bottles (deposit 3d[1]) by rubber-stamping a letter 'B' for Burton on the label, a chore that had to be performed every time there was a delivery. This could not be done for milk bottles (deposit 1d) as they had no labels, and this gave rise to an incident that my brother, sister and I laugh about still. A customer produced an empty milk bottle and my father refused to take it. She insisted that she had bought it from us and flew into a rage, at the climax of which she whacked the bottle down on the counter. To my father's surprise and, no doubt, relief, it didn't break but merely rolled onto the floor at my father's feet; so he got the bottle without parting with the deposit on it.

Right from the start, I liked being in the shop. On the first days there, we children thought that just about everybody who walked on our side of the street would enter and buy. They didn't, of course, but somehow the family survived. Even after I went to Hymers College at the age of 11, I

---

[1] 'old' pence.

still found serving behind the counter more enjoyable than doing my homework. Because we were the cream of those who passed the Eleven-Plus examination, the 20 or so scholarship boys, of whom I was one, tended to perform better academically than the fee-payers, most of whom had come up from Hymers Junior School.

There were often errands to be done for the shop, though my father never imposed on me in that respect. Some of these involved local suppliers. Sometimes it was a matter of taking a petrol can round to Ellyard's the funeral directors, just round the corner, to buy a gallon of petrol which my father put, with the required measure of oil, into his two-stroke BSA Bantam motorbike. The only person I ever remember seeing at Ellyard's was a taciturn man with a face lined by chain-smoking in the manner of W. H. Auden; he looked as if he might become one of his own customers at any moment. Another port of call was Sam Batte's, to carry home half a stone or a stone of carrots or onions if we ran out of them in the shop. Sam Batte was essentially a potato wholesaler, but the potatoes, being so much bulkier, were delivered to our shop by lorry. Then there might be magazines to buy, of which my father read quite a few, or his pools entry to take to the post office. The magazines were a weakness of my father: each week he took—at the same time, as far as I can recall—*Answers*, *Everybody's*, *John Bull* and *Competitor's Journal*, whilst his daily fare was the *Daily Express*, which was very jingoistic in those days, and the [Hull] *Daily Mail*. The Sunday papers included at least the *News of the World*.

My father dealt with several wholesale grocers, the activities of any of which would have been dwarfed by the volumes of goods dealt with nowadays by a single supermarket branch. His main wholesaler for many years was Hull Supply Company in Blanket Row. Their very personable and amusing traveller, Norman Dee (whatever were his parents thinking of?), used to call on my father every Monday morning. Once business had been done in the shop, he would come through to our living room to drink tea and tell funny stories for a long time. It was from him that I first heard the cornflake joke ('I'll tell you the rest next week, it's a cereal'). Eventually, Mr Dee took another job far away, and my parents were hurt that we never heard a word from him again. Another caller was Mr Bursall, a burly traveller from Bower & Thorley, I think, though I may be muddling wholesalers up now. Yet another grocery traveller was John Barnes, of Johnson's, always very smartly turned out in hat (was it a bowler?), crisp white shirt and dark tie. The jars of boiled sweets were delivered by his humorous and quick-witted namesake Johnny Barnes, who, with his elderly mother, also made them all. How I wish I had seen his factory, full of equipment that by rights should later have gone to a museum, but was probably simply all thrown out. Angela did visit and can recall the aroma of the sweets to this day. Other sweets and so on came from Coote's on Spring Bank; Cyril Coote had lost the sight in one eye after a rose thorn entered it.[1]

Other errands involved going into town on the number 70 trolleybus, perhaps to buy cigarettes from Koplik's in Mytongate, or from W. H. Smith's wholesale showroom (at first in a partly-blitzed building in Jameson Street, but later in newly-built premises behind the bus station). As cigarettes are so heavily taxed, this involved taking substantial sums of cash, which I always took great care to keep safe.

During those years at 4 Strickland Street, my mother had, as far as Angela and I can remember, three women who came to clean. First was Mrs Crellin from the next terrace down (if you look at the 1881 census, you will see that more or less everyone with that surname comes from the Isle of Man); not long after we moved there, her husband had helped my father make and fit a new counter top of wood and hardboard. Then there was Mrs Moore, Angela recalls. She lived in about the third house from the top of the street on the east side. Her husband had been a boxer and had a boxer's nose. Mrs Moore had several sons; on at least one occasion a younger one, Stephen, came with his mother and sat in the living room while she worked.

The third helper was a lovely little round lady called Mrs Smalley. Her husband was a cobbler, who kept a little shop near Cave Street on the west side of Beverley Road. She was a cheerful, intelligent and humorous soul, and we were all sad when a few years later, she died of cancer.

The kitchen at 4 Strickland Street had one piece of equipment that must have been very high-tech when the house was built: a range with a side oven. Though we had an ordinary gas oven, the side oven came into its own before Christmas: my mother often claimed that Christmas cakes and fruit cakes never cooked better, and if anyone knew, she did. In any case, it would have been wasteful to light the kitchen fire other than in the winter.[2]

On a hook in the yard hung the 'tin' bath. This was manhandled into the kitchen when necessary, and hot water heated on the gas stove in a large preserving pan. Later a gas 'geyser' was installed over the sink in the yard, which made life easier. I remember once saving time by using my sister's (broken) hula hoop as a hose to take the water directly from the

---

[1] Harry Davill a policeman friend called regularly, and parked his helmet on a chair whilst chatting with Dad. *AEH*

[2] Historical note: Open fires for cooking gave way to complicated ranges in Georgian times. In about 1770, in the north of England, one of the iron panels at the side of the grate was replaced by an iron oven, directly heated from the side of the fire. However, this tended to cook unevenly. A more expensive type was developed with flues running all round the oven and thence up the chimney. (Adapted from an article in the *Mendip Messenger*, 23 November 2005.)

geyser to the bath—the idea worked beautifully. Sooner or later the welded seams of the bath would start to leak, and I suppose we got through several baths whilst we lived at our off-licences at Strickland Street and, later, Constable Street.

There is one episode I often call to mind, perhaps because it was so uncharacteristic. Prompted no doubt by sixth-form physics lessons at school, I once found myself in a brief discussion with my father about why the planets revolved around the sun. To his mindset, their motion required some constant power. In vain I pointed out that they went round the sun because there was nothing to stop them. As soon as the words were out of my mouth, I realised that this was a concept he would never be able to grasp. It makes you realise how revolutionary Newton's ideas—of force, of action and reaction—must have been in his own day.

When we lived in Strickland Street, some of those who lived near us were very poor by today's standards. Many were incapable of imposing any sort of order on their lives. I dare say many of them were unemployed for all or much of the time. One such was Mrs Wainfer, a youngish woman who lived on 'our' side of Thorne Terrace, on the south-east corner of which stood our shop and house. She had a little girl, whom she used to bring into the shop with her. The girl often demanded to be bought one of the sticky cakes we sold, which were displayed, covered by a sheet of cellophane, on a tray on the end of the counter. The mother's reply was invariable: 'You're not 'aving a bun. Yer've gorra bun in 'ouse' (this was untrue). Tragically, when the girl was 15, she was murdered in the Old Town. The case received wide coverage, not only in the local press but in the national press too, not least because the body was found in the curiously-named Pig Alley. In spite of intense police inquiries over a long period, which included exhaustive tracing of foreign seamen who had been in port at the time of the murder, nobody was ever brought to book.

When the girls who lived around us left school at 15, they often went to work at Smith & Nephew, about three streets away, where Elastoplast was made, or at Rosen's slipper factory on Hessle Road. The boys often became 'deckie learners' on the trawlers, though I remember that Father once encouraged a lad who had just taken a job on the railway which he was not enjoying, and with good reason. The first jobs these youngsters were given included cleaning out the fire-boxes of steam locomotives.

There was another off-licence on the Hessle Road corner of the street, on the east side; in the 1950s a couple called Jackman took it over. Fixed to the house next door—that is, in the street itself—was a war memorial for the street; I believe they are called 'street shrines' nowadays, though there was no religious message on ours. Some other streets in the neighbourhood had these too, carved in stone. But Strickland Street's—more evidence that poor people lived here—was of wood, at eye level, with several columns of names neatly painted in small black capital letters on plyboard. It must have been glazed at one time; if so, the glass had gone. At any rate, the plyboard was exposed to the elements and the plywood was curling. Poor though the people may have been, the mindless vandalism that is such a feature of life 40 years later, was absent, otherwise the memorial would never have survived as long as it did. All the same, at some time when we lived there it eventually disappeared altogether. Many of the streets off Hessle Road were demolished in their entirety: what, I wonder, happened to the memorials that were still intact? There is now (1994), I believe, a book about Hull's street war memorials.

On the corner of the terrace opposite stood another grocery shop; unlike our shop it was not an off-licence. It belonged to Matthew Westerman, a Jew known to all as 'Jewy'. As well as his wife Cissy, his father also lived with them when we first moved there, and spent much time standing at the door of the shop (the surest way for a shopkeeper to deter prospective customers, I've always thought). From time to time, a drop would form at the end of his very Jewish-looking nose and eventually fall, hence his nickname of 'Dewdrop'. He died after a few years. Later Cissy's sister Lily, from Leeds, used to come to stay for long spells. Then sooner or later, Jewy and the two sisters would have a row and the women would rush off up the street, bra straps hanging out of their suitcases, to jump on the trolleybus, take the train from Paragon station[1] and make their escape to Leeds for a while. All this was wonderful entertainment for us from our vantage point behind net curtains opposite; we did not actually know the Westermans in any way, for the two shops were in deadly competition with each other. How Matthew Westerman made a living is beyond my comprehension, as my father, I suspect, had enough trouble doing so, especially in the earlier years at Strickland Street, and Jewy didn't even sell alcohol. Perhaps my father's income improved later when people became rather better off as post-war austerity gradually receded (though by then we children must have cost more to feed and clothe). It was also known that Matthew Westerman was a gambler who frequently went off to play cards with his cronies—though goodness knows what he used for money. Cissy did, however, give our family a wonderful catch-phrase. On the only occasion I ever remember her coming into our shop, it was to buy a tube of glue. But not just any old glue; the question she kept repeating to my father was, 'Have you got any wood glue?' We hadn't; it was one of the things—and there weren't many—that Father didn't sell. But to this day, if anything needs mending my brother, sister and I are liable to cry that what's needed is wood glue!

---

[1] Paragon station is now called 'Hull' as there is no longer any need to distinguish it from all the other railway stations Hull used to have.

There were one or two other shops further down the street. Walters' was one, and I recall another on the south-east corner of the street; but they were not such a competitive threat to us. (If you look at a map, you will see that the name of the street that runs along the south end of Strickland Street is Goulton Street, but it was always known as 'Bank' because in the 19th century it was indeed the bank of the Humber before land was reclaimed for the railway yards.)

There were many other characters that my sister and I can call to mind from those years. In the warmer months, Mrs Cropp could be seen in the terrace opposite weaving trawler nets, using hooks set into the house wall for the purpose. Several houses had these hooks. In our own terrace, Mr and Mrs Smith lived next door to us, and their young son would often come into our shop, where he had the mannerism of swaying from side to side. This was merely one of the innumerable foibles of our customers that we secretly mocked in our living room behind the shop. Further down lived Mrs Lewis, a trawlerman's wife. In around 1954, my mother, who was nothing if not kind and thoughtful, sent my sister and me down to give Mrs Lewis a pair of baby's socks (we sold those too), for she had just given birth to her ninth child, and there indeed lay mother and new-born baby. I have no idea where the other eight children were, as the tiny house could surely not have been big enough for all of them.

An occasional customer was a toothless and consequently very thin-faced woman aged perhaps 35 or 40, Mrs King. Like many of the women in our neighbourhood, she was old before her time, but in her case there was good reason. It was said that once a boy was knocked down and killed in the street outside the fish-house[1] where she worked. She ran outside to help and found that he was her own son.

Around the middle of the far side of Thorne Terrace lived a shrunken, smelly, old couple. Eventually the wife died, and to the surprise of all, Mrs Kell, a cheerful, stout, motherly widow who lived about three doors further down the terrace, married the widower and took care of him from then on. Mrs Kell was definitely one of the cleaner types around there; some of the inhabitants, indeed, were quite houseproud. But often the houses were completely unkempt and stank to high heaven, so much so that it was almost nauseating to walk through the front door and hit the fetid miasma. In the years since we lived amongst these people, Alec Gill[2] has written accounts of the lives of families of Hull trawlermen. Gill's research is sincere and fascinating, and gives a far broader picture of the fishermen's lives than the partial one we saw. We did not sentimentalise those times, as they were the years of our upbringing. We observed Hessle

[1] Fish-processing factory.
[2] Alec Gill and Gary Sargeant, *VILLAGE WITHIN A CITY: The Hessle Road Fishing Community of Hull*, Hull University Press 1986, ISBN 0 85958 450 X.

Road life at first hand from our standpoint behind the shop counter. We did not attend school in the area, so our friendships were made elsewhere, but we had priceless experiences which we often recalled later in life.

None of the customers had a telephone, of course, so ours was used for emergencies; my parents never stood on ceremony in that respect. One evening—I suppose I was about 12 years old—the hospital phoned and I answered. Would I tell Mrs So-and-so in Such-and-such Terrace that her baby had died? Shocked at having this task thrust on me, I went through to the shop and told my father. At that moment, a girl came in to buy something. She lived in the terrace in question, and to my relief my father gave her the job of passing the message on.

Kell, and other Strickland Street surnames that I can remember such as Beaumont, Blenkin, Feetham, Gill, Hessey, Lupton and Usher, may be old Hull names, as they can all be found in the parish registers of St Mary's, Lowgate, around 1800.

By 1962, Hull's slum clearance programme had reached Strickland Street, and with many houses around us now empty, a couple of days after Christmas we moved from 4 Strickland Street to 6 Constable Street, a few hundred yards away and on the north side of Hessle Road. There were a few snow flurries that day. I missed the actual move, as I was at work at City Engraving.

More of life at the shops[1]

At the Strickland Street shop, the till was an unlocked drawer under the counter. It had a wooden bowl for coins and a space behind for bank notes. I do not think we were ever robbed. Dad paid his suppliers in cash, and banked the takings once a week. At the end of each day, he totalled up the takings and put all the money in OXO tins, which he took upstairs. When Auntie Laura (my mother's sister) visited, she jokingly asked Dad whether his OXO tins were full! We could hear and see customers, as there was a bell on the shop door and a mirror on the wall so that we could see into the shop from the house. At busy times, there would be a shout of: 'Can somebody help, please?' from Mum or Dad, and one of us would go to serve.

Customers' notes (often ending with 'Much obliged') were sometimes perplexing, and we all attempted to translate them. Dad had fun with messages relayed by children. One child insisted on asking for: 'half a pound of large'. When Dad asked if it was lard or marge (margarine) that was required, the word 'large' was reiterated. Dad had to guess and hope that the item would not be returned. Potatoes would be requested with an emphatic: 'Mi mam wants big uns for chips.' (My mother would like some big potatoes to make chips.) Dad's stock response was 'Ah, but who's

---

[1] Written by AEH.

going to buy the little ones?' When he had sold out of broken biscuits, a wag would declare: 'Well, I can always break some for you!'

Running up a bill at the shop was normal practice. Most accounts would be paid off at the end of the week, but there were defaulters who would avoid our shop for a while. Mum was good at asking for money, as she had collected rents for her father years earlier. She was also firm in refusing a person credit, and on more than one occasion she berated Dad for allowing a poor payer to start another account. On pay day, she would knock on a debtor's door and ask for half-a-crown or two shillings towards the bill. When the debt was paid, the customer returned to trade with us. By then they had perhaps run up a bill at another shop further down the street.

Mum had a sideline, trading at Myers wholesalers in Waterhouse Lane. She would take customers' orders for clothing, shoes and small household goods. Items came on approval and were paid for in instalments. Later, when she did not see the clothes or shoes that she had sold, she speculated that they had been 'hocked' at the pawnbrokers.

Although we always had a washing machine (I remember a square ADA machine with a wringer at the back), the laundry van called, especially in the winter. Bedding, table linen and the pale brown shop coats that Mum and Dad wore were whisked away. Later in the week, the clean laundry, wrapped in brown paper and tied with string, would appear on the front doorstep.

One night, Dad was woken by a moving light at the bedroom window. On looking out, he discerned a policeman with a torch. After some muttering and disturbance of the household, he hurried downstairs, fearing a broken window or even worse, a break-in. What had happened was that during his regular patrol, the constable had almost fallen into the shop when trying the door handle. Dad had forgotten to lock it. After a chat and a cheery 'Goodnight', Dad made the shop secure, and all was well.

Our early-morning alarm clock was the clattering echo of the fish workers' heavy clogs on the pavement, as they hurried to start their morning shift at the nearby fish-processing factories. Some women worked in the smokehouses, and had yellowed hands from the dye. Plenty of fish was given to us: at times, there were two or three parcels of cod in our big fridge in the shop. Any visiting friend or relation would be the lucky recipient of one of them.

When the fishermen came home from their hazardous three-week trips on the trawlers, they donned their unique pale blue or pale grey suits with bell-bottom trousers and pleating across the back of the jackets. Taxis were hired, and they would tour the pubs and clubs, or take their families on spending sprees. On one occasion, I remember a fisherman's wife buying wallpaper paste from the shop, as she was decorating a room late at night ready for her husband's homecoming.

On Sundays, the Salvation Army Band played in the street. The ladies' tambourine technique was imitated by young onlookers. At other times, a man brought a horse pulling a roundabout. Eager for a ride, children would persuade their elders to give them a few coins for this treat. The rag-and-bone man, with his horse and cart and his often imitated cry, was also a regular visitor. Children received a balloon or a goldfish in return for donations.

Moving house or, to use the Hull term 'flitting', was sometimes undertaken on handcarts. 'Moonlight flits' did happen too, said to be the means of avoiding the rent.

An occasional cat fight flared up between two female neighbours. Suddenly a cacophony of shouting was heard. In all probability, the protagonists would be friends again the next day.

Some residents did not venture far, and it was believed that some old people had never moved more than a few hundred yards from their homes.

Mum was a great help to the local people. She assisted with sewing jobs and gave advice on cooking. One day a man rushed into the shop, his top half clothed in just a vest, and his face hidden under shaving soap. He spluttered that he wanted to buy a towel. Mum told him that we did not sell towels but asked him to wait. A minute or so later she handed the man a towel from her own linen cupboard.

When the Strickland Arms, almost opposite the shop, showed the door to its customers at closing time, drunks would weave their way down the street. When we wanted to pass, a game of chance ensued in judging the direction in which they would lurch next. In their wake, children gathered up the coins that had been thrown down or spilt from their pockets.

In our house, preparations would be made for the chimney sweep's visit. The room was cleared, and what was left was covered in dust sheets, for soot easily spread. During the operation, someone had to go outside to report when the brush could be seen poking out of the chimney. For those who did not employ a chimney sweep regularly, there were chimney fires. Excited crowds would gather when the fire engine arrived. Similarly, when an ambulance appeared in the street, a crowd soon assembled and formed an untidy guard of honour around the house until the patient was brought out on a stretcher. Our parents told us that it was rude to stare at people's misfortunes, and news from customers or a glimpse from behind the net curtains had to satisfy our curiosity about street events.

When we moved to the first shop, we continued to attend our C. of E. primary school, St John's, Newland, which was on the other side of the city. That meant four trolleybus journeys, or eight buses per day if we went home for lunch. The latter arrangement involved a lot of running. Later, at secondary school, we had no such choice, as there were other buses to catch and lunchtime activities to attend. We were sometimes teased by other children in the street, as we were regarded as 'posh' in our respective school uniforms. Once or twice I had to run the gauntlet of taunting, and I broke the school rules by stuffing my school beret in my pocket for the last few yards. However, these occasions were rare, as the family was respected and we got on well with people.

The contents of the shop mirrored the seasons and religious festivals. Jimmy Almond delivered fruit and vegetables in season. We sold firewood and firelighters all year, for it was in the days when every house had coal fires and regular coal deliveries. We stocked Christmas cards and decorations, and Dad took orders for presents such as toys, as well as Christmas cakes and puddings, boxes of chocolates and biscuits. In addition, a bigger range of alcohol was ordered. At busy times, every corner of the shop overflowed with stock, and it spread into the house. We had a Christmas club into which people paid what they could afford. This was mainly for orders for poultry, which duly arrived from the farm of Dad's good friend, Laurie Caley. At Christmas, Mum's orders from the warehouse had a welcome boost. In October, we stocked fireworks ready for 5 November. I recall that Dad kept them in old biscuit tins and always seemed glad to have sold them. For Easter, we had a selection of Easter eggs and chocolates, most of which were special orders.

In the vicinity of the shop, celebrations and times of mourning were marked in special ways. Christenings took place at the non-denominational Fishermen's Bethel or at the C. of E. St Barnabas Church. Babies were dressed in elaborate christening gowns embellished with lengths of blue or pink ribbons. When grief struck, as it often did in the fishing community, black arm bands were worn. There were several occasions during our years at the shops when trawlers and their entire crews were lost at sea. At these times the whole community would be devastated, but would come together to help the families who had lost loved ones.

Life's tapestry

After several days in agony, my father died of large bowel cancer at Hull Royal Infirmary, Anlaby Road, on the morning of Sunday 17 May 1981. The hospital telephoned us as soon the hour was decent. We drove over there—presumably Angela drove and took Mother, Roger and me. They had placed him in a side room but I did not want to go up to see him. My mother did. When she came back down, she said only, 'I kissed him'. I think I then walked to St Mary's, Lowgate, which was my spiritual home in so far as I had one, where the service had just finished. I'm not sure if people became aware that I had just been bereaved, but if they did, they did not know what to say.

The funeral at St Mary's a few days later was followed by cremation. In the back pew was a knot of sad men who had been his friends at the allotments on Kenilworth Avenue.

On Sunday 2 May 1982 both my sister and I were staying for the weekend at my mother's at Chadcourt, Hull. On the Sunday afternoon, Angela drove me to Western Cemetery (on the corner of Spring Bank) to show me the family grave, which I had never seen before; I had not been present when my father's ashes were interred there. Either before or after that, we also drove down Fountain Road out of curiosity to see the cemetery where my Grandfather Burton is buried, picking our way over the overgrown extent of it on the north side of the road, and noting the lack of gravestones, before making our way back to Chadcourt and describing our expedition to Mother. When the weekend was over, Angela returned home to Doncaster, and I to London.

When I left, probably on the Sunday evening, Mother made a point of kissing me goodbye, which was out of the ordinary since as a family we were not always demonstrative in that way. My mother died suddenly and alone the following Friday morning, 10 days before the first anniversary of my father's death. A next-door neighbour found her. It is true that she had suffered from angina for many years. Nevertheless, given all the circumstances and that she probably only had to stop taking the drugs prescribed for her heart condition to bring on a heart attack, there must at least be the possibility that her dying at that time was not wholly coincidental. However, she never gave the slightest hint that she was tired of living. She was a very gracious and gentle lady in her old age, yet hated being old, not only because of the disability which her heart condition brought—when she was out of doors she had to stop every few yards before she could go on, especially when the weather was cold—but because she thought that she looked old.

My sister Angela was married to Christopher Harris at St Mary's, Lowgate, Hull, on Easter Monday, 27 March 1989. I, as a Vicar Choral at Wells Cathedral [see page 58], was put in charge of the music, and promptly delegated the task to Frikki Walker another Vicar Choral, so he and I chose the music together. The pipe organ at St Mary's was unplayable, and the only alternative at that time was a two-manual Hammond electronic with two octaves of pedals, so I thought it best to concentrate on the singing.

After all the Good Friday and Easter singing at Wells, soon after evensong on Easter Day I was driven up to Hull by Lyndon; Robert made his own way, and Frikki and Christine Walker drove from London where they had been singing that day at St Cyprian's, Clarence Gate.[1] We all stayed for two nights at the Valiant House Hotel, opposite the Cecil Cinema on Anlaby Road. On the Monday morning Frikki and I went down to the church so that he could familiarise himself with the Hammond organ, and the rest of the quartet joined us later.

The wedding of Angela Burton to Christopher Harris, 27 March 1989
L–R: Gerald, Geoffrey, Pamela (his wife), Christopher, Angela,
Roger, Shigeko (his wife)

Before the service, a quartet consisting of Frikki's wife Christine (soprano), Lyndon Pullen (an alto who sang at Wells for 25 years, until Christmas 1988), Robert Rüütel (who had recently joined Wells Cathedral choir as a bass Vicar Choral) and myself, sang *O sing joyfully* (Batten), *Jubilate Deo* (Lassus), *Cantate Domino* (Pitoni) and *Exsultate justi* (Viadana). During the opening hymn *Let all the world in every corner sing*, the bride was escorted up the aisle by Uncle Henry. (He and Gladys were married at St Mary's in 1938, as my parents were in 1936.) There were four other hymns. Angela's friend from college days Anne Paskett (née Bennett), then a deacon, read the lesson. During the signing of the register the quartet sang the *Sanctus* from the *Requiem* by Fauré, and *Laudate Dominum* by Mozart, and for the recessional *The Lord bless you and keep you* by John Rutter. Then Frikki played the Hornpipe from *Water Music* by Handel.

The one thing that inexplicably went wrong was that not one of St Mary's little choir turned up at 12.30 p.m. as arranged to practise with us—the plan had been that they would help us to sing the Fauré, the Mozart and the Rutter, as well as the psalm, number 121. Now I knew

---

[1] Gerald's wedding present to the happy couple was bringing the musicians. *AEH*

that Gordon and Cynthia Robinson wouldn't be able to make it, as their house at 69 Swanland Road, Hessle was the base for the bride and bridesmaids. But why the rest refused to join in I still don't know! However, the quartet coped.

The sun shone just long enough, and apart from the church choir's absence, everything went without a hitch. I was pleased to see Roger and Shigeko in the congregation. The quartet and some of the church choir retired to Ye Olde White Harte in Bowlalley Lane afterwards before the quartet went back to the hotel, where the reception took place with about 100 guests. There were speeches by Uncle Henry, the bridegroom, Angela herself and the best man. In his speech, Henry referred to the fact that all three of our family's marriage entries are in the same register, as only about 240 couples had been married there in just over 50 years.

Reflections on some Hullisms

Hull has many dialect words. I was reminded the other day, by a press report about a Glaswegian accused of murdering his baby son, of the verb 'skelp'; this is used in Hull (though as it is low-class slang, we ourselves did not use it), and means to hit, slap or beat. A word with the same meaning is 'clatter', as in 'If you don't behave I'll clatter you.' In a tribute to the footballer George Best in the *Daily Telegraph* on 25 November 2005, Michael Parkinson, who is from Barnsley, in an amended version of an article he wrote in 1999, said: 'At Highbury, Peter Storey awaited, at Chelsea, 'Chopper' Harris clattered all comers.' My cousin Christine told me that older women in Hull can (or could) be heard disparaging other women they consider frumpy, using the word 'nunty'. A Holderness word that our farmer friend Laurie Caley would have used is 'galluses'—braces, the things that hold your trousers up.

My father's mother, Grandma Burton, called a clothes-horse a 'winteredge' ('winter hedge'), though this was a West Riding usage, as she was born at Birstall. And a word my mother sometimes used—she always laughed self-consciously when she did so, knowing how funny it sounded—was 'ewkered'. This referred to some gadget, a pair of scissors for instance, that had been broken or bent so that it was unusable or wouldn't work properly. (Since writing this I came across a very similar word in a list of Devon dialect words; could Mother's 'ewker' have been handed down from her Devon-born father's father?) 'To rive' is a Hull verb, and means to pull at something clumsily, with the danger that you will break it: 'Don't rive (at) it'. (In St Mary's, Lowgate, parish registers for around 1780 you will find entries with the occupation 'lath river', rhyming with 'diver'.) As many people still do, my father used 'back end' to mean late autumn, especially when talking about what needed doing on his allotment. Children were 'bairns', though again this was not a word that we used. In Hull it is pronounced 'bains'. Other words that the people we lived among used, but we did not, was the verb 'to chow' (rhyming with cow), meaning to shout at or berate somebody, as in 'If I don't do these errands me mam'll chow at me', and the adjective 'lairy', meaning cheeky, impudent—Christine heard it in 2006, for the first time in years. Very recently I mentioned, in Somerset, that something had got 'taffled up' and was met with a blank look. In Hull, it is used of a jumble of wool or string that needs unravelling. Conversely, there were words that were never used by Hull people: 'huge', 'fetch' and 'mislay' were three that I only learnt to use later in life.

Christine points out that 'syrup', as in Lyle's Golden Syrup, is always 'treacle' in Hull.

Holidays[1]

The holidays of my childhood always took the form of two weeks at the seaside. The earliest I remember were at Filey, then there was a long series at Scarborough, and in my teens, one or two at Whitby.

Gerald and Angela, Scarborough, *c.* 1952

[1] The first two paragraphs of this section are written by GDB, the remainder by AEH.

My mother was once well and truly outraged at Scarborough. She took me (and my sister, I think; I am not sure where Roger was) to the cricket when I was about 10 years old, but the gateman didn't tell her that the match was likely to end at any moment, and there were no refunds. However, she did point out a spectator to me (perhaps on that occasion, possibly on another), though how she knew who it was I do not know. I don't suppose I paid much attention, but the man was Wilfred Rhodes (1877–1973), one of the greatest cricketers of the 20th century. The first test match he played in was W. G. Grace's last! Rhodes would have been nearly 80 when I saw him. Though he had been blind for a number of years, he claimed to be able to follow everything from the sounds.

Scarborough, 1945
L–R adults Lilian (Gerald's mother), Gladys (Uncle Henry's wife),
Ada Reed (Gladys's mother);
on laps Gerald, Robert and James (twin cousins);
in front Roger and Richard (cousin)

When we were small, we spent family holidays at Scarborough with other relatives. Two families plus some grandparents rented a large house. On the train journey, the babies had to share their normally spacious baby carriages with tins of food and dried goods. Later on, after Dad took over the first shop, he was unable to leave it for even a day, but always made sure that Mum and we three children had our two weeks' summer holiday. On Thursdays, half-day closing, he made the trip to Scarborough on his motorbike for a brief visit before returning to open the shop for evening trading. We stayed in bed-and-breakfast accommodation, and our day-time base was one of the many beach-side bungalows strung out along the North Bay. Sometimes we had a pitched-roof chalet, and at other times one with a flat roof which was good for playing ball games, until the ball flipped over the edge. Each chalet was equipped with crockery and cutlery, a kettle, table and chairs, deckchairs and a little cooker. We had lunch and tea there, presumably shopping on the way to the beach.

Days were spent in the hot sun (or so it seemed), and pocket money went on donkey rides, swing boats, boat rides, rides on a mechanical elephant, beach toys and horse riding. We spent most days on the beach, with trips to the nearby open-air swimming pool. Other treats were rides on the miniature railway and the splash boat. We savoured ice creams at the Corner Café or at Scalby Mills. Today's children would be surprised that these were our only experiences of eating out. Evening trips were to the cinema, variety shows, the illuminated woodland walk in Peasholm Park, and the Open Air Theatre. We were not usually allowed to go to the amusements at the south beach, but one day Gerald came back with a big grin and a pocketful of money, as the machine had paid out.

On the mechanical elephant, Scarborough, 1951
A safer way to travel?
L–R: Gerald, Angela, Susan (cousin), Roger

Later, when we were older, we stayed in Whitby, out of reach of Dad's weekly visits. However, during the year he treated us to days out, and included us in his sea-fishing trips at Filey and Bridlington.

During several summers we enjoyed visits to my mother's sister Laura and family in Eastcote, Middlesex; from there we attended London theatre performances such as *My Fair Lady*, and BBC live broadcasts.

Gerald and Roger, Scarborough, 1999

Hymers College, Hull

Years after I had left Hymers, I compiled in my head a list of all the boys in my form. This is the first time I have written it down (May 2006):

Allison (whose father was something in the fish trade), Christopher John Atkin, Martin David Barrett, William E. Blackburne (whose father was a surgeon), Burton, Christopher Culpin (a small boy who lived at North Ferriby), Curtis, David Dagwell (whose father ran a ropery, if I recall aright), Doyle, Evans, Gatie, Goldberg, Greensmith (whose father had a stationery business in Story Street), Harris (a member of the Plymouth Brethren), Harrison, King, Geoffrey Lipman, Meggitt, Milner, Morgan, Cavan O'Brien, Rodney Pickering, Karlis Edgar Prams, David Procter (a good cricketer), Robson, Malcolm Roeder, David Saward, David Stothert, Thompson, Weston and Donald Winter. This list of 31 names does not quite match the normal class size of 29, as a few boys had moved forms or left the school; I remember that Harris moved with his family to Liverpool. I do not remember the Christian names of all 31, but some of the missing ones were doubtless called David, which was an extremely popular name at that time.

Name of Scholar	Date of Birth	Name of Parent	Occupation of Parent
O'Brien Cavan Andrew Gerard.	23 July 1945	O'Brien Kenneth Leoner	Headmaster
Overton Geoffrey.	8 May. 1944	Overton William Edward	Assist: Cost Accountant
Procter David Charles	1 May. 1944	Procter Lawrence -	Aircraft Designer
Richardson James Stuart	12 Nov: 1943	Richardson Neville Ashton	Bank Official
Searson Hugh Mager	21 Feb: 1944	Searson Arthur Roy.	Bank Clerk
Sims Geoffrey Malcolm	29 Aug: 1944	Calvert Noel (stepfather)	Fish Shop Proprietor
Waudby Edward John	22 Sept 1943	Waudby Grace (Mrs)	Postwoman
Weston Arthur Henry	31 May 1944	Weston Betty Hutt (Mrs)	Secretary
Atkin Christopher John	8 May. 1944	Atkin. Benjamin	Bank Manager
Barrett Martin David	3 June 1944	Barrett Ronald James	Chief Pharmacist Hull Infirmary
Burton Gerald David	17 June 1944	Burton Basil Blagham	Grocer
Dagwell David	24 Dec: 1943	Dagwell Alfred Roland	Company Director
Evans, Erik Howard	26 Aug: 1944	Evans Wesley Emlyn	Salvation Army Officer
Gatie Brian Anthony	20 July 1944	Gatie. Henry Anthony	Newsagent & Tobacco
Goldberg, Thomas Guy	18 Aug. 1944	Goldberg Woolf	Research Chemist
Harris John, Philip	31 Oct: 1943	Harris Ralph David	County Supplies Officer
Lipman Geoffrey Hyman	28 June. 1944	Lipman Maurice	Director (Outfitter)
Lomax David Malcolm	12 Sept 1944	Lomax Colin Malcolm Stafford	Assist Operating Supt: British Rlwys
Pickering Francis Rodney	13 May 1944	Pickering Frank	Head Teacher
Prams Kârlis Edgars'	2 April 1944	Prams, Arvids	Chief Accountant
Robson, Brian Henry.	3 Oct: 1943	Robson Henry	Clerical Assist

An entry in the register of Hymers College, Hull

Gerald managed to remember an impressive
proportion of these names [see page 29].

ADDRESS	LAST SCHOOL	Entered in Form	Left in Form	Date of Leaving
"Polar Chalet" South Cliff, Bridlington	Helstuthorpe Junior Bridlington	L3C		44
37, Sunningdale Road, Hessle	Hessle C/E	L3B		44
"Inglea" Skillings Lane, Brough	Elloughton C.P.	L3B		44
66, Station Road, Hessle	Hessle C/E	L3B	IVB	3-9-58 44
233, Kingston Road, Willerby	Carr Lane, Willerby	L3B	IVB	25-5-58 44
4, Meadow Close, Beeford	Beeford C/E	L3B		44
Northmoor House, West End, South Cave	South Cave	L3C		44
40, Newgate Street, Cottingham	Cottingham C.P.	L3B		44
26, Auckland Avenue, Hull	Newland C/E	L3A		44
175, Marlborough Avenue, Hull	Bricknell Avenue	L3A		44
4, Strickland Street, Hull	St John's C/E	L3A		44
188, Victoria Avenue, Hull	Bricknell Avenue	L3A		44
64, Schmers Avenue, Hull	Thoresby Street	L3A	V3A	31-10-56 44
62 Hartoft Road, Bricknell Avenue	31st Avenue	L3A		44
212, Park Avenue, Hull	Bricknell Avenue	L3A		44
248, Park Avenue, Hull	Bricknell Avenue	L3A		44
30, Northfield Road, Anlaby Rd Hull	Wheeler Street	L3A		44
942, Anlaby High Road Hull Fassignoe House, South Milford, Leeds	South Milford	L3B		44
28, Highfield, Sutton on Hull	Cavendish Road	L3B		44
41, Pearson Park Hull	Park Road	L3A		44
13, Claremont Avenue, Fountain Rd.	Fountain Road	L3A		44

[Continuation of facing page]

There were three Jewish boys, who loitered in the corridors during daily (Christian) assembly and only joined the rest of us for the headmaster's announcements: they were Goldberg, Greensmith and Lipman. After we had taken our 'O' levels in 1959, we were divided into the sheep and the goats: the sheep being those who did 'A' level arts subjects, and the goats those who did science subjects.

The number of schoolchildren studying science has fallen greatly in recent years, but even then, on balance, the arts side had the edge in terms of boys' aspirations. Christopher Atkin, however, who had by far the finest intellect in my year, studied maths in the sixth form, later gaining a place at Christ's College, Cambridge (and a PhD somewhere else). Rodney Pickering, who I would say was runner-up in the intellectual stakes, studied arts subjects and took philosophy at university. When I last met him, in the 1970s, he was teaching philosophy at what was then the North London Polytechnic.

Maureen Lipman says of her brother Geoffrey in *How was it for you?*: 'My elder brother was a natural athlete who excelled at anything from bowling alleys to rugby union. In fact he had his nose broken so regularly in the scrum that he ended up with a retroussé. No mean event in our family.' He is a lawyer and a prominent figure in a number of world travel and tourism organisations.

Christopher Atkin had been a great friend of mine at St John's, Newland. He was an only child. His mother Molly was a schoolteacher at Beverley Road School, and his father the manager of the Hull Savings Bank branch on the corner of Beverley Road and Pendrill Street, and later a bank inspector. During his career he had accumulated an assortment of curious English coins, notably a two-headed Victorian penny.

At St John's, Christopher had taken the new *Eagle* comic, in which the lead cartoon story concerned Dan Dare who was pitted weekly against a green extra-terrestrial creature called the Mekon. Not surprisingly, Christopher's playtime fantasies—certainly when he and I were seven years old—centred on spaceships and space travel, though I always seemed to remain behind at the launch site—the space craft must have been rather small. His later study of mathematics was wholly consistent with those games.

Martin Barrett was also at St John's; we became friends again at Hymers, having parted company at the age of seven when he changed schools. It was through him that I learnt to play the cello—after a fashion. Our teacher was a kindly fellow called John Keenan [see page 36].

Because my GCE 'O' level results at Hymers were judged to be poor, my wish to study arts subjects in the sixth form was ignored and I had to do science and maths. It occurs to me 46 years on that this was iniquitous. If there was a greater demand for arts subjects than science, the school should have made some of the science staff redundant and employed more arts staff. (Think of the money they would have saved! No more expensive laboratories, just a few extra textbooks.) So I spent two bored years in the sixth form, and still managed to get 'A' level passes in Chemistry and Maths for Science (in 1961). At that point, the school perpetrated another swindle at my expense. Nervously, I went to see the Headmaster, Mr H. R. Roach—the only time I ever met him on a one-to-one basis—and told him I thought I ought to leave and get a job. He dissuaded me. I was too trusting; it was years before it dawned on me that the only reason he would have done that was so that the school would not lose the fees paid by Hull Corporation. Consequently, I whiled away a year redoing the failed Physics 'A' level, to no purpose whatsoever. Does all this rankle still? You bet! Still, I'm reminded of a remark my mother made once or twice, as if she were looking at an old school photograph: 'There's teacher, she's dead.' Most of the time I tried my best to take in the science that was being taught, and have found the essence of it invaluable in making sense of the world later. (And had I not had some grasp of mathematics, I would have had unimaginable difficulty with the quantitative side of the London Business School MSc course 10 years later, always assuming that I would even have been offered a place at the outset.)

Hymers College, Hull

At least I passed Physics the second time around. Heaven knows what I did the rest of the time, though a German poetry class took up some of it. This was strange, as I knew no German. Still, the class was enjoyable, there was no exam to worry about at the end of it, and we were taught—if that is the right word for such informal sessions—by the gentle and humorous Mr Mitchell, who happened to be the husband of the Mrs Mitchell who had taught me at Newland Infants School 10 years earlier. I remember that we read a poem by Christian Morgenstern, about a man who catches a mouse and releases it in a remote forest.

Six generations of the Harrisons[1]

Maggie and Jack Harrison were our elderly neighbours when we were small children and living in Hardy Street. They would look after us when we were ill and our mother had to go out. Later in life we realised that we remembered more about their living space than our own. Jack would produce a set of dominoes with coloured dots. They were kept in a black fabric bag hanging in the cupboard in the living room. On other occasions Jack would be knitting socks on four needles. It was a skill that many seamen had in those days. He smoked a pipe. Jack had a workshop at the rear of the house, where he made wooden toys for us, including a dolls' house and a garage. Toys were scarce after the war, so we were lucky. On ironing days Maggie would use heavy flat irons that were heated in turn on the gas ring in the little kitchen. There was a fringed chenille tablecloth on the table. Fitted to a stout rail behind the living room door was a heavy patterned curtain that was raised when the door opened. The room was heated by a large cream-coloured cooking range that had a fire going all day.

Our parents were friends of the old couple, and we visited Maggie in an old people's home on Cottingham Road after Jack died. Their son Arthur, an engineer, had migrated to New Zealand in the 1920s with his wife Hilda and young son Norman. The New Zealanders came back to visit in the late 1940s and early 1950s, when it took weeks to make the journey by sea. I remember meeting Hilda in the early 1950s. Norman told us years later that he used our telephone as his grandparents did not have one. More than five decades later Gerald and I were welcomed into the homes of Jack and Maggie's great-granddaughters in New Zealand. So how did this come about?

Between those times, our family had kept in touch with the old couple's son Arthur, his wife Hilda and their son and daughter, Norman and Brenda. Every Christmas we looked for the letters and cards from three households in New Zealand, and treasured the exotic stamps and the occasional photograph. After our parents died, a trickle of correspondence developed into a steady flow after new relationships were established. We found we had much in common with the new generations of Harrisons, and firm friendships were established with Norman and his wife Valerie, and with their daughters Eleanor and Susan. On my first visit

[1] Written by AEH.

to New Zealand in 1987 I met the Hilda from my childhood once again. By then she was in her 90s. Subsequently, we welcomed various members of the Harrison family into our homes, and they entertained us in New Zealand. We shared holidays in both countries. Their visits to Britain included Hull and, in particular, Hardy Street. On one notable occasion, the then resident of 96 Hardy Street allowed Eleanor and her husband, Bob, to tour the house where Maggie and Jack had lived. Eleanor saw the room where her father, Norman, had been born, and I returned to the room where I had played with the coloured dominoes all those years before.

Gerald and Angela, New Zealand, 2002

When Gerald and I visited New Zealand in 2006, we realised that we had met six generations of Harrisons. Norman, grandson of Maggie and Jack, was a great-grandfather by then. We owed much to our parents' neighbourliness.

John and Molly Keenan

The Keenans lived in a Victorian terraced house at 69 Spring Street, in central Hull, demolished in the 1960s. Molly was blind. Their daughter had died at the age of 11 or so. A year or two after I left school they held a party for their friends—perhaps it was an important wedding anniversary. In the course of it Molly sang 'What is life' from Gluck's *Orpheo ed Euridice*. I found it an extraordinarily affecting performance.

A little after that they moved to a little house in Beverley, where I resumed my cello lessons, though with a little more application than before. John had two or three cellos; the best was one which had lost much of the wood outside the purfling. I often wonder what happened to it; it must be somewhere. John was good enough to go to Leeds and buy a cello on my behalf from Balmforth's, a very well-known firm in its day. It cost £50 and is perhaps worth about £3000 now (2008). It was not until 2007, however, that it became more playable: I took it to Kai Roth near Shepton Mallet and he pointed out that the strings were too far from the fingerboard (making it very hard to play). He adjusted that and fitted a set of new strings.

The Caleys[1]

Throughout my childhood, we kept in touch with Laurie and Dorothy Caley, who were tenants of a 126-acre mixed farm a few miles east of Hull at Smithy Briggs, near Sproatley, on the Burton Constable Estate. (Briggs is a northern version of 'bridge'; there is a little bridge over a stream near the farmhouse.) My father had come to know the Caleys when he collected milk from farms during the Second World War. They must have hit it off, and the two families have stayed in touch ever since. During the war, my father delivered the Caley boys to their school during his rounds, and if he was late, so were they. At that time, his lorry could be searched for 'contraband' acquired in the country. He did not risk the offer of farm goods, as the penalties could be severe. I visited Smithy Briggs several times as a boy. How could one ever forget the vast teas prepared and spread out in the parlour by Laurie's wife Dorothy? In earlier days, the farmhouse was lit by oil lamps, and there was no flush toilet. The latter toilet was fitted in about 1948 and electricity was installed in 1951. Dorothy admitted to lighting the oil lamps out of sheer habit until she became used to the new marvel. Laurie and Dorothy had three children, Cedric, Jack and Wendy. Laurie died in his fifties in 1962 and Dorothy aged 88 in 1992. Cedric died in 1998. There are many fascinating stories to record (and sad ones: foot and mouth disease broke out on the farm in 1944 and 1947).

---

[1] This section includes recollections from members of the Caley family.

Roger worked at the farm as a schoolboy in his teens. He was told that in the 1930s, before Laurie had a car, he had a pony and trap; all their relatives in that area used that mode of transport. An uncle of Wendy's had such a rig, and on occasion, hopelessly drunk, drove it into the middle of a pond.

As a young man, Laurie lived at a house called *Twisted Chimneys*, at Marton. A photograph of this house with its chimneys is in the Abercrombie Plan of Hull (1945); but it was knocked down long ago. Laurie was courting Dorothy, née Porter, who lived at West Newton Grange. One evening he had travelled to see her in his pony and trap, on which he had placed the candles required for night-time driving. However, there had been a lovers' tiff, the subject being Dorothy's new short hair style, and he was late leaving. On the way home, he was woken from his slumbers by the police, as he had no lights visible on his cart. Laurie had to go to court and was fined £1. The magistrate said: 'I find it disgraceful that a tenant of mine is out and about at 1 a.m.' He did not seem bothered about the lack of candles. Ironically, there were spare candles in the bottom of the cart, but Laurie had not thought to replace them.

Laurie went into farming in 1923. Ploughing was done with horses until about 1942. Roger remembers the tack still hanging up until about 1960— if it had been kept oiled and in good order, it would be worth a fortune today. There was much more dairying early on, but after the foot-and-mouth outbreaks, Laurie no longer kept dairy cattle. Instead he had suckler cows, sheep, pigs, chickens, geese and turkeys. He fed the turkeys on eggs and nettles. In those days, the profit from 200 hens paid the men's wages and the household costs.

Angela used to stay on the farm during the summer in the 1950s. There was only room for a girl. She used to collect the eggs and on one occasion was handed a live chicken by its legs. She was told to take it to the farmhouse. She ran like the wind, gripping the flapping bird's legs tightly, before being relieved of it by a waiting Dorothy. She was staying there when a straw stack fire broke out in the farmyard. The first that was known was the reflection of the flames in the window. Then the fire engine was summoned. Jack said he had never descended a stack so speedily! Angela remembers that after a hard day's work, the Caley brothers devoured whole pies that had been baked that day. She recalls travelling on a trailer to take lunch to the workers who were busy harvesting. Vivid are the memories of playing among the stooks of corn, typical of those days.

Laurie and Dorothy combined sheep-buying with annual holidays in Scotland. They would send a telegram to say how many sheep were to be transported by train from Kelso. This was so that Cedric and Jack knew when to collect them from New Ellerby station, and thence with the help of dogs to escort them by foot to the farm. In this way, the flock was replaced over a period of about three years.

After we moved to Strickland Street in 1952, Laurie called on us every Monday afternoon, having been to the cattle market in Hull in the morning to jaw to his friends, whether he had been selling any beasts or not. Generally on these occasions, a sack of potatoes would be brought into the shop, Laurie would be paid cash out of the till, and he would then ease his bull-necked frame into the armchair in the living room, between the door into the shop and the understairs cupboard. Tea and cake would be served, and the events of the week mulled over. The approach of half-past-five meant that it was time for him to leave us to collect Dorothy and Wendy from their regular weekly shopping expedition into Hull. The rendezvous was always Hammond's car park in Ferensway. Reluctantly easing himself out of the armchair, Laurie would don a collar and tie, which he had earlier deposited in a jacket pocket. The whole ceremony was accompanied by much muttering. As far as I know, this was the only time of the week these items were worn, but it was more than his life was worth to turn up at Hammond's without having duly placed them around his protesting neck.

When Strickland Street was being demolished in 1962, Cedric and Jack bought from the demolition firm some of the cast-iron lavatory cisterns, complete with ballcocks, and they installed these to supply water in their pig houses back at Smithy Briggs. We thought it a very ingenious and amusing piece of farming. Jack later told Angela that the idea was entered in a Young Farmers' Rally competition for inventions.

Concerning potato-growing at Smithy Briggs, Roger told me that a woman who lived on West Parade in Hull used to organise a gang of pickers. On arriving at the field, it was the practice to bargain (with Laurie and Cedric in this case) to fix the picking price per row. The gang organiser would pace out the field, for of course the rows of potatoes on one farmer's field would not be the same length as those on another. This canny woman and the farmer would agree a deal, and work began. It was customary for each picker to be allowed to take home as much as she could carry at the end of the day's work, perhaps a hundredweight. Cedric drove a van to carry the pickers, with a bale or two of straw in the back to serve as seats. This was fine in the morning when the pickers were taken out, but not so comfortable in the evening, as by then the van's load had more or less doubled![1]

———

[1] The remainder of this chapter is written by AEH.

In the early 1980s, Gerald helped with reading and copying the historic diary and writings which Dorothy Caley had inherited from her uncle in the 1950s.

In 1910, Dorothy, aged six, was taken to Canada with her sister to be brought up by her uncle, Jack Cookson and his wife Jessie, who had no children of their own. She returned to work on her parents' farm in East Yorkshire in 1919. We were fascinated by the events in the diaries, just as we had been by Dorothy's tales of life in pioneering Canada. Dorothy told us that their timber house had an earth floor, and almost everything had to be made. She described how the horse pulled a cart in summer, and a sledge in winter. She learned how to cook and to make butter then. On visits to Smithy Briggs many years later, we savoured her home-made butter and delicious baking.

Her uncle, Jack Cookson, had left for a new life in Canada in 1890, and the handwritten diary provides an account of his uncomfortable and eventful voyage from Liverpool to Halifax, Nova Scotia. He wrote of sleeping in a hammock in the cramped and sometimes dangerous quarters on board the *S S Polynesian*, a sailing steamship with three masts, carrying 1100 people. He described the conditions on board, comparing crowded and dangerous steerage quarters with the luxurious saloon. During the voyage, the ship struck a small iceberg, the winds tore a sail, 24 bunks collapsed, and he lost his precious 'yankee' hat overboard. At first eating was impossible, but after he found his sea legs, additional food was obtained by bribing the stewards. At the end of the voyage, a cargo of brown sugar had to be mixed with what little coal was left, to get them into Halifax harbour. Jack boarded a train to go west and told of crossing ravines on trestle bridges 'which did not look over-strong'. However, the train was warm, with tea and food supplied. The train had two engines which were 'throwing snow off the rail with the cowcatcher'. An Indian boarded the train with a collection of furs to sell further along the line.

When Jack claimed land to develop, he sent to England for his fiancée, Jessie Porter. Other family members also made the journey. There are reminiscences of his early years there, taking jobs on the railway, farming, brick-making and panning for gold, prior to his settled life of service to the community in Tofield, south-east of Edmonton. He had hair-raising journeys fording rivers and crossing frozen lakes with his horses and carts, meeting Indians who later sold out to the settlers, and learning how to live from the land, forests and lakes. He built a stable before his first cabin, for horses were essential work partners. He developed the land and built a homestead, subsequently working in farming and mining. Gas was discovered under his land, and Tofield became the first town in Alberta to have street lighting. He shipped a piano and organ from England and was a stalwart of the growing church community and the school board.

These writings shone a light on pioneering days in Canada. They were scrutinised by Gerald who then made copies, and a bookbinder was engaged. Later, Gerald painstakingly prepared a transcript of the pencilled diary of the voyage and of the later stories and reminiscences. The typed document and a book of the copied originals were lodged with the Archives department in Edmonton, Alberta.

2

Moving On

Gerald's computer log shows that he began typing his autobiography a few minutes after midnight on 7 May 2003 (probably on returning from the pub!), and last worked on it on 19 May 2008. Sadly, his cancer prevented any further work, and he died three months later.

Using much of Gerald's own writing, his sister Angela E. Harris now fills in some of the rest of his life story. Given his sense of humour, perhaps the following pages should have been given the subtitle: *For The Life Of Him…*

Living the life

From his family roots in Hull, Gerald moved to study and work in London, where he took advantage of all that the city had to offer. From the late 1960s to the middle of the 1980s, he experienced the best in art, theatre, cinema, concerts, jazz, choirs, opera, ballet, BBC recordings and much more. He took our parents to famous theatres, and obtained tickets for memorable productions involving some of their favourite performers. However, within his vast experience, not all was to his liking. In 1974 he commented on a soloist at the Queen Elizabeth Hall: 'Imagine a bespectacled barrel draped in gold lamé.' Fortunately for her, we have no report of her name or of her singing ability.

Gerald described a concert at the City Temple, with the esteemed Eric Thiman at the organ. He wrote: 'What a thrill to hear John R. Watkinson's *Lift the Strain* sung by a choir that was bigger than the audience.' John Watkinson was the brother of Len, who had been in the choir of St Mary's in Hull when Gerald was a choirboy there.

Gerald's musical life developed alongside his academic one, as he became a willing piano accompanist, played the organs at several churches, and sang in greater and lesser venues in the capital. He wrote about high jinks at Bedford College (London) in 1971:

> Tonight I've to go back to College to sing in a quartet at the farewell concert for the principal. All we have to sing tonight are extracts from the College rules to Anglican chants; we are to be introduced as Bedford College's answer to the 'Joy Strings'[1]—the 'Misericords'.

After five years at university, in 1973 he obtained a job as a corporate account manager with National and Grindlays Bank (later Grindlays), and bought a ground-floor flat in Gloucester Terrace, London W2. Prior to

[1] A Salvation Army music group.

this, he had tried to study independently, unsuccessfully as it turned out. He wrote of his early academic struggles:

> In 1966 I ditched my little printing business [see page 53], and pigheadedly decided to stay with Roger at 80 Ranelagh Road, Ealing, London W5, teaching myself German and music. In 1967 I rashly sat 'A' levels in these subjects. Needless to say, I failed. At last I found that Hull College of Commerce would take me with open arms—like a Sixth Form College. From 1967–8 I studied French, German and British Constitution there and bagged three more 'A' levels. These took me to Bedford College (then in Regent's Park), London University: no wonder—there were only three main-course students in Dutch Language and Literature in my year. I took over Roger's bed-sit in Ealing for £5 per week. Students in small departments tend to get higher-class degrees; I got an Upper Second.

Gerald and parents at his BA graduation, London, 1972

The residents at Ranelagh Road were very well fed, as the landlord's brother was a caterer to the rich and famous, and delicious leftovers were distributed and eagerly consumed. Gerald recorded: 'Dai left me a good half pound of lovely roast pork and the greater part of a rhubarb pie.' This food supply must have been most welcome to a student. Whilst in Ealing, he much enjoyed events at Ealing Green Church. For instance, he helped with technical terms for a poem for a retirement dinner: 'We got the metre and the rhymes more or less right and then they set it to a plainsong tune on the organ ready to sing to some unsuspecting retiree.'

Gerald's organ-playing in London brought in some money. Like his father, he had always found ways of supplementing income. As a boy he used the window of Dad's off-licence shop to trade his stamp collection, and children used to peer through the glass prior to entering the shop to choose stamps from the sheets displayed there. He earned money as a choirboy, with extra coins in his pocket for singing at weddings and funerals. Later he had a small income from playing the organ at St Saviour's Church in Hull. When at university, he typed essays for fellow students and never paid a penny for his own typing. He even earned money for library duty at university, and wrote: 'With my organ-playing cheque for the term, (£18[1]), doing the typing (£4) and library duty last Saturday, income seems to be making a better effort to catch up with expenditure.' On his summer university placement in Dublin, he earned money for a job well done, being rewarded with 10 weeks' pay for 9 weeks' work, no doubt a banker's bonus of the day.

Gerald had some unusual experiences in his London days. In 1973 he toured Bolsover Colliery in Derbyshire with a group from the London Business School, and told of having to sign forms indemnifying the National Coal Board for anything that might happen to him. He wrote:

> We all had to carry a rescuer, essentially a gas mask that stops you breathing in carbon monoxide by converting it into carbon dioxide.... Then everyone found the polythene sack with his name on it, containing all the clothes to be worn; underclothes, blue shirt, boiler suit, socks, boots, helmet, leather belt and thick rubber knee pads. We went off to the large locker room, trooping into the attendant's office on the way to collect our keys.... Having changed, we headed for the lamp room. The miner there was very helpful, and we soon got our rescuers and our lamp batteries buckled onto our belts.... Instead of clipping the lamp onto our helmets immediately, most of us held them until we needed to use them down the pit. When you need to put the lamp on, you take your helmet off and tie the two ties at the back of it so that the wire from the battery to the lamp runs tidily up to the back of the helmet, and then round the side of the helmet to the lamp itself. The lamp is housed in a thick rubber casing, or it would soon get knocked to pieces as you banged your helmet on things. The lamps have two bulbs in them, a bright one and a dim one. The helmets were sturdy and made of plastic but very light.
>
> The lamp man gave each of us two numbered discs, a square one and a round one, made of brass.... Our guide held up the netting whilst we entered the cage, and as we did so we gave up our square tallies to the banksman, the cage operator, who communicates to the winding man … and we fastened the round tallies to a clip on our batteries. We were frisked for cigarettes, matches or lighters before getting into the cage. The cages carry both coal and men so you have to stand on or in between the

[1] In the late 1960s.

rails that bear the coal tubs when they're in it. They run the cages at a lower speed when people are in them.

So then the cage is fastened, and suddenly it's moving downwards. After two or three seconds, your stomach lurches as the cage reaches its maximum speed.… It's pitch black, as nobody's lamp is on, and you are going down into the teeth of a tremendous gale, because you are travelling against the ventilation flow. It takes a long time before the cage begins to slow down, and you wonder if it ever will.

The tour of the mine shafts followed. There was a brisk walk of two miles to the coal face, following the roadway which held the conveyor and a set of rails down one side. The floor was covered in a thick white substance. After watching a couple of different methods of coal cutting, we eventually arrived at the main face. The face is 200 yards long … and is cut by two shearers, enormous machines, each of which cuts half the length of the face. The shearer is pulled along by an enormous chain, under which a steel sheet moves to take away the coal tumbling down from the shearing blades. A jet of water is sprayed onto the blades to keep the dust down. When the shearers have traversed the nearly 6-feet-high 200-yard-long face, the hydraulic roof supports are moved. The roof is supported by these steel supports, like enormous jacks—two at the front and one at the back. By operating these, the miner takes support away from the roof and the support then propels itself forward.… Then another bit of roof is jacked up. When this rank of supports has been moved forward, the shearer cuts a new swathe.… Bits of roof might fall in front of the supports, but the miners stay among the supports; so it was like working one's way along a low colonnade about 4 feet 6 inches high. Behind the supports, the roof collapses. The face moves forward 16 feet a day so … that one face produces about 2000 cubic yards of coal a day. As the face moves forward, the roadways are lengthened on the left by a cutting machine, and on the right by blasting and shovelling the coal out with a hydraulic shovel. This is because of the ventilation flow; the air is travelling from right to left, and blasting produces less dust. The roadways are 10 feet high and about 15 feet wide, but in many places the enormous weight of the rock above has made them start to cave in; it's quite awesome to see how substantial girders can be twisted into grotesque shapes. About 80 of the 700 workforce reconstruct subsiding roofs for the passage of the conveyors, coal tubs and men.… Remember, everything in the pit has to be taken down in a size small enough for a cage, to be assembled down below.

The worst bit was when we had to crawl about 20 yards to get from the roadway to the face on hands and knees, (which is where the knee pads came in useful) with a gap of about 2 feet 3 inches from the floor to the coal ceiling. We watched full tubs of coal banging empty tubs out of the coal cages, to be taken up to the surface … it was like a fairground switchback, complete with 'creepers' to pull the tubs up slopes and give them energy to career round the corners to the cage if full, or to the loading point if empty.... Back at the top we were shown round the washing and grading plant. All the coal and rock come up mixed together … and water is used to separate the two.... All the coal goes to power stations, and for this they use railway wagons. Still it was lovely coal and would have done just as well as house coal. Overlooking the colliery is Bolsover Castle, over which Cromwell is supposed to have fired a cannon, hence the name! They aren't allowed to mine under the castle, or under the local church, for fear of subsidence.

All the coal was mined mechanically; what can't be got out by machinery is left where it is. There are conveyors for carrying men as well as coal, as the distances are so great; we jumped on one as we were returning to the bottom of the shaft. At the end of it there is a little station platform, so you have to look sharp to jump off neatly. In all, we were underground for three hours. The miners were very friendly, and were interested to find that we had never been down before. We were glad to use the pit showers when we reached the surface. Tired but clean again, we set to work on a great spread prepared for us; chicken legs, trifles, Newcastle Brown and Mansfield Pale Ale, etc. Having thanked our guides … we went into the town, where we continued our relaxation at the Miners' Welfare Club.... A few of our party played snooker on a well-kept table. We set off back to Regent's Park, getting there at midnight.

Another journey was memorable for different reasons. Gerald is the only person I know who had to escape from an aircraft by an emergency chute. He was flying back to Dublin in 1973, on his placement as part of his business degree. A bomb scare was announced, but the captain said it was probably a hoax. The passengers were told that on landing, they had to escape by the front exits. Gerald wrote that the pilot managed to bring the aircraft to a halt in half the length of the runway and quickly turned onto a slip road:

> I was soon off sliding down the inflated chute. We had been told to leave our hand luggage behind, but some silly people didn't. One woman asked me to pass her coat but I refused! As instructed, we got quickly away from the aircraft and into waiting buses—there were four fire engines and an ambulance there too—which took us to the buildings. Our baggage was subject to an indefinite delay, an hour and a half in fact, so I had a free snack, and at noon all the passengers were taken to the plane to identify their luggage. Then luggage and passengers were taken back separately to the terminal before being reunited. The hoax got four inches in that evening's *Herald*.

A sequel to the experience was that his appointments at the bank that afternoon were running late, as two men had been delayed by a bomb scare! This experience did not put him off flying, as his many subsequent flights demonstrated.

Travel featured highly in his life. He spent a term in Holland at the University of Leiden as part of his studies, and made lifelong friendships there. Subsequently, he had an abiding love of Holland and its people, culture and history. Whenever he grasped the opportunity to visit galleries in foreign parts, he sought Dutch art, as he had a good knowledge of that too. During his time in Leiden, he was living in a former hospital building, and noted that the student warden, himself a poor postgraduate student, sold the lead on the doors of the old x-ray department, as he must have needed the money.

Flea market, Amsterdam, 1985

Gerald's musical travels were extensive: competing in musical festivals at home and abroad, and travelling with several choirs around the world. His trips to Rome and Brazil with Wells Cathedral Choir were particularly memorable [see pages 65–66]. He was also busy with trips to Australia and many European countries, with the London Chorale and the English Concert Singers. On the Australian trip, the packed itinerary 'put the aspirin consumption up' as he described in a letter. When living in London, he visited the Holy Land with members of his Ealing church, and visited the historic sites with a group of people who would remain his friends for life. He was an ideal travel companion, interested in art, history, architecture and much more. His friends and relatives invited him for holidays in France and elsewhere. He was good company, witty and interesting, but at the same time self-contained and could occupy himself, reading or studying a musical score or two. He loved wine and wineries, and visited more than a few in various countries.

Gerald visited Japan twice on the invitation of his Japanese sister-in-law, Shigeko. With her help and that of his brother Roger, he soon became absorbed in Japanese culture. He enjoyed all aspects including the food, and especially the travel by the Bullet train.

Railways fascinated Gerald; he was a member of the West Somerset Railway, a preserved line near where he lived in Wells. He delighted in taking visitors on this line, usually fitting in a walk and a lunch in Minehead.

He was always busy, often hurrying hither and thither, singing, playing the organ or piano, earning a living in various ways, and pursuing his numerous hobbies. He was a detailed planner and record keeper, and was well organised. However, on one occasion he overslept when Wells Cathedral Choir was due to board a coach to London for a recording. He sped down Vicars' Close, apologised to the waiting choir and officials, and prepared to travel by car to the London venue. With some luck, he arrived in time, and no harm was done.

In contrast, back in the 1970s, after a job interview in Holland Gerald must have set some sort of record by travelling on 13 vehicles in one day, including perhaps the fastest aircraft boarding time ever:

> I was given a lift to the station, thence by train to Utrecht and the KLM bus to Schiphol. Here the fun started; I got out of the bus at 8.04 p.m., knowing that every minute counted since the flight was at 8.15. The passport control officer said I had to check in, even though I had no hand luggage; again, fortunately there were hardly any other people around. Having checked in, I raced past the passport officer who recognised me this time as a mad Englishman, and just waved me through. At the top of the passage to the aircraft, I amused the security staff as I hunted for my boarding card while they searched my briefcase and checked me in the security scanner; as soon as I was in my seat they took the boarding tunnel away, the engines screamed, we taxied a short distance and we were away.... Back in London, I took a bus and two underground trains. In total, I had used four underground trains, three buses, two planes, a taxi, a car and two ordinary trains. That makes 13 vehicles, on 13 November.

After gaining his first degree Gerald applied unsuccessfully for several jobs. However, there was one academic institution that beckoned. He had eyed this institution in Regent's Park for some time, never imagining that he would be welcomed over its threshold. He related:

> I applied to the London Business School on the off-chance. (London Graduate School of Business Studies is its full title.) Part of the admission procedure is an aptitude test. I turned up at the University and joined a long queue. A booklet was issued, which took us three hours to work

through. I had a headache for hours afterwards. To my surprise, I was called to a further interview, and was asked what I thought of my score. However, it had not been posted to me as it should have been.[1] I found it was 713 and only one person had scored more.

According to correspondence at the time, a perfect score is 800; scores of below 300 or above 700 are rare; the students at the London Business School have the highest average score of any such institution, including Harvard; the average for 1st year students of the MSc course at London is 633. Gerald continues:

> I could have practised on past papers (which presumably others had done) but it never crossed my mind. I believe my score put me in the top 1% of all those who took the test in business schools worldwide. For the first time in my life, I realised that I had a brilliantly quick brain—there's modesty! So I sailed in!

There was also a selection day with an interview and competition for 20 places from the 45 candidates that day. So, much to his delight, from 1971 to 1973 Gerald was the recipient of a Social Science Research Council grant, and had a room in the residence wing of the London Graduate School of Business Studies. He commented: 'Who wouldn't like a room overlooking Regent's Park?' He felt very lucky to be a student there for two years, and gained his MSc in Business Studies (equivalent to an MBA). He made many long-term friends there as he had done at Bedford College, and as well as concentrating on his studies, he joined the various musical and social groups on offer.

Gerald had been recruited as a piano accompanist at the Business School, and it was in this capacity that he took part in *The Hollow Crown*, an anthology in drama of speeches, documents and music associated with the British monarchy. It is described as 'a mixed evening of readings and songs by various authors including the monarchs themselves'. He wrote:

> *The Hollow Crown* involves the most work for me, as I've some hard things to play on the piano—an electric piano is being hired, so that a harpsichord effect can be produced as well. All I knew before we arrived at a house in Chelsea, was that we were going to give a studio performance. So the cast of 10 duly turned up, where in the studio at the back of the semi-basement there was an electric piano, hired for the evening to simulate a harpsichord, a Bechstein grand piano of fairly old vintage, but still very good to play, several microphones, and, in a closed-off section, a big tape recorder which could be operated by remote control from the studio side of the glass.
>
> Any bits we were not happy with could be retaken, so we weren't as anxious as at the live performance (which had taken place the previous

---

[1] The letter about the test arrived a month after its American postmark, as the postal district had been omitted from the address.

week). The moving force behind the enterprise seemed to be one of the students on the Sloan programme (at the Business School); he and his wife seemed to live in the house. However, our host and hostess seemed to be another couple, Lord David Dundas[1] and his wife Corinna, who is a model at the Lucy Clayton Agency. The whole place could be summed up as trendily utilitarian. Still I didn't mind, especially as there was a table covered in bottles of wine and spirits and plates of smoked salmon rolls and things.

Interestingly, on the publicity for *The Hollow Crown* in the college newsletter, Charles Handy's name is below Gerald's in the cast list. Handy was joint founder of the London Business School. He was a professor there for many years, and his publications will be familiar to those who have studied organisational behaviour and management. I note from the newsletter that admission to the performance was 20 pence, and that there was a wine bar!

Gerald's interest in history was satisfied in London, and he delighted in historic finds. In 1969 he wrote:

> I discovered Marylebone High Street after I'd walked down Baker Street. Elizabeth Barrett and John Browning were married at Marylebone Church, and Charles Wesley lies buried there. Dickens wrote six of his best books when living in a house on the corner of the High Street and Marylebone Road.

Gerald had many similar experiences and knew London well. He made a point of studying the interiors of London pubs, at least that was *his* reason for sampling the beers!

In 1975 he was marginally involved in the Balcombe Street Siege. This was an incident involving the IRA and the police in London after a bombing campaign. There was a six-day siege when two hostages were taken and held in a flat. The siege ended with the surrender of the four IRA men and the release of the hostages. The events were televised and watched by millions. 'The Balcombe Street gang' had fired gunshots through the window of Scotts restaurant in Mayfair. After being spotted and chased by police, the four men ran into a block of flats in Balcombe Street, triggering a stand-off. The inspector involved in the chase, John Purnell, was awarded the George Medal for his bravery, and several other officers were decorated. The gang surrendered when they heard on the radio that the SAS was to be sent in.

An unsuspecting Gerald was nearby when the siege was starting:

> I got into the Portman Arms just after nine o'clock on the evening it started, and was well on with my meal when lots of people came into the basement from the bar upstairs. I thought, surely there isn't room for all

---

[1] David Dundas made records in the 1970s and 1980s, notably the catchy *Jeans On* in 1977 which had started off as a jingle for Brutus jeans. He appeared on *Top of the Pops*, and later became known for film and television music.

these people to eat, and it was 10 minutes or so before the diners realised that the bar had been cleared, because there was thought to be an armed man in a flat opposite. After false hopes had been raised once or twice, eventually the police announced that we could leave two at a time. I was about the first to go up; they told me to keep right down as soon as I got to the top of the stairs, then to turn left out of the door, still keeping down, and to run for 20 yards. I stayed in Gloucester Place for about 10 minutes, and there were police cars and Land Rovers and ambulances everywhere, with Dorset Square cordoned off with white tape, but I didn't hang around long.

Gerald's London life brought him in touch with well-known people. When he first bought his flat in Gloucester Terrace [see page 56], yachtswoman and authoress Clare Francis lived in the house. Members of the cast of the television programme 'Allo 'Allo! frequented his local pub, and he would spot newsreaders and other familiar faces on his travels around the capital. He recalled that on arriving at a performance of Godspell, he found himself next to John Betjeman. Numbered among the speakers at the Business School formal dinners were Harold Wilson and Enoch Powell. Gerald wrote that 'he had a very good seat' for the latter. In 1975 he wrote about an experience with the St Mary's Singers, a group based at St Mary's, Bryanston Square, where he sang in the church choir and sometimes played the organ:

> Last Saturday was the nicest day I'd spent for a long time. [The singing group rolled up at a house in Oxfordshire, and had drinks and food in the garden.] Our car-load was welcomed by the cousin of one of the two sisters who own the house; only later did I learn it was Hardy Amies, and he came to the concert later.

Gerald suggested to the conductor that Hardy Amies was looking at his suit, whereupon the inside of the jacket was displayed to show a label that said 'Styled by Hardy Amies'.

On one of the Welsh trips with the London Chorale in the early 1980s, the choir won three classes in the eisteddfod competition, and subsequent revels extended into the early hours. Gerald related that the last competition did not finish until midnight, after which wine was drunk. At 1.30 a.m., they were told that the pub was open: '... but the Chorale people down there couldn't sing, as there were no tenors. Off we all rushed, four tenors in one car, and we left the pub at 4.10 a.m.—the dawn chorus was well begun.' Sleep was not a feature of those trips, as breakfast was at 7.30.

Gerald had a knack of making friends throughout his life. People liked his gentle wit, his modesty and his helpful ways. He made many enduring friendships. He had time for people, however busy his day, and rarely uttered adverse criticism of others. During his university placement in Dublin, he wrote that he did not hit it off with someone 'but that largely through my pliability we had reached a modus vivendi'. He became enthusiastic and knowledgeable about Wells Cathedral, and friends and relations were treated to his tours. He was generous with his time, and at various stages of his life, had encouraged learning in others, teaching English and maths, bookkeeping, harmony, and keyboard and organ skills.

He related well to older people. He learnt this from his mother, who visited elderly neighbours with a child or two in tow. When a young Gerald was late for tea one day, his excuse was that he had been in an elderly neighbour's house waiting for the cuckoo to come out of the clock! Gerald kept contact with his teachers and mentors, his university professors and, of course, his older relatives. He was a good neighbour to Bertha Barber, an old lady who lived in the flat below him in Vicars' Close during the years when he sang in the cathedral, and also later when he moved to No. 10. They had their Yorkshire roots in common, and Gerald would provide company and help in return for TV viewing.

His singing went from strength to strength, as he undertook a wide variety of choral and solo engagements. He suffered a setback in 1991, when he had an operation to remove an acoustic neuroma. He had lost the hearing in his right ear just a few years into his spell of singing at the cathedral. Remarkably, once recovered, he adapted well, and much of his best singing took place after this episode. He resumed singing in the choir as if nothing had happened, and 'plough on', as his friend Robin Rees quoted, was the order of the day.

With Jane Isaac at the surprise 60th birthday party, 2004

Gerald celebrated significant birthdays memorably. His 50th birthday was spent in a Somerset brewery. We know what his friends would have called it, but all the jolly attendees were still vertical when the photographs were taken. His 60th birthday party, a gift from his close friend Jane Isaac, was held in one of his locals near Wells (he had several) and he had no idea that 'a meal' was really a big party. His face was a picture of surprise, captured on camera. Many of his friends were there, including his long-term Business School pal and erstwhile chess opponent, Chris Coggill, who had travelled from France.

After moving to the West Country, Gerald continued to attend music and theatre performances. Once, after attending the theatre in Bristol, he and a friend found themselves walking in step with a person whom they had just seen on the stage. There resulted a spirited conversation with, as Gerald recalled, an extremely charming Barry Humphries, who was walking back to his hotel.

Gerald's tastes in entertainment were many. He never owned a television, but he loved the cinema and would recommend films he had seen, especially when living in London. Having a lively intelligence, he appreciated the wit of others, and especially liked the black humour of the Ealing Comedies. Latterly he encouraged us to see the film *Hot Fuzz*, which had been filmed in Wells, disrupting the place for a while. He registered equal delight in a side-splitting *Ken Dodd Show*, as he had done many years earlier in a performance by the pianist Artur Rubinstein, both with Roger. His musical tastes ranged from his beloved church music to jazz and opera. He loved the theatre, following our mother's example, as she was a regular attender at the New Theatre in Hull.

Gerald did not participate in organised sport other than at school, but he loved to watch cricket. He followed Somerset latterly, and went to watch matches with his friends. There was a memorable occasion when he was on holiday in New Zealand. By a stroke of luck, England were playing New Zealand, and Gerald was able to accompany our Wellington cousin Richard Acey to the match. Gerald was puzzled to see young men carrying battered settees into the ground, until he realised that this unusual furniture removal was the New Zealand fans' way of ensuring comfort whilst watching the match.

Printing as a hobby and a business: 'Types and shadows'[1]…

If you ever saw Gerald peering quizzically at some print but not reading it, he would be looking at how it had been printed, because he had been a printer. Print and printing interested him throughout his life. I think he liked the precision that printing offered.

In his mid-teens he bought an old printing press, and started printing small items such as concert tickets. It was an interesting hobby, and must have made him some useful money. During his final illness, he wrote:

> At age 16, printing had become an enthusiasm. I bought an 8-inch by 5-inch 'Cropper' treadle press. After pacing up and down for ages outside a typesetter's, there I entered and begged some type from the receptionist; it must have been the Hymers uniform. Next day, a case of 10-point Times Roman was delivered to 4 Strickland Street. I spent the next year or two buying minimal quantities of type and turning out all manner of tickets and leaflets for friends, and made a few shillings. This continued after we moved to 6 Constable Street. Somehow my printing machine was moved too, and I soon had the three sections bolted back together—the platen itself, the stand, and the flywheel. The first of these was the heaviest, and my teenage muscles strained to lift it up all the stairs to the attic.
>
> Later, probably in 1966, I decided that I needed to go to university, and my little printing business had to go. I sold the machine for £10 to my cousin Rob Barnes, who wanted it for the school where he was teaching at the beginning of his career in education.

Gerald kept the Hull musical fraternity well supplied with handbills and tickets. He learned the printing technicalities of the day via his Letterpress printing methods. He printed for organisations of friends and relatives, as well as for weddings and other celebrations. Appointment cards, headed stationery and business cards were produced. He stretched to printing St Saviour's Church magazine, and work for other churches. He printed for Hymers College concerts and built up a list of clients.

His musical performances early on were accompanied by his printing skills, as he printed the tickets and the handbills. He printed for the lunchtime concerts at St Mary's, Lowgate and, no doubt, helped with distribution. Dad and I helped him with the ticket-numbering device, and Dad's excellent parcel-wrapping skills came in useful.

In Dad's first shop, the printing press was at the back of the kitchen, and at the second it was in the attic. I can still imagine the sound and the feeling of the rhythmic 'thump, thump' as the press turned out tickets and handbills one at a time. Gerald gradually learned about type faces and sizes, and also the sizes of paper and envelopes. He made useful contacts with

---

[1] From the hymn: 'Now, my tongue, the mystery telling' (*'Pange, lingus, gloriosi Corporis mysterium'*), St Thomas Aquinas, 13th cent.

suppliers, and scoured the trade papers for his requirements. He made a sample book so that he could discuss orders with customers.

Letterpress printing was labour-intensive, as each piece of type had to be selected and set in the correct position. Having learned about typesetting, Gerald became a compositor, placing type from where it was stored in the wooden cases (now often used to display wine corks). He would set the type into lines of the same width, and tie the finished 'job' or page with page cord ready to be transported to the printing press on a galley, a flat metal tray on which to slide the type. Spaces would be filled with pieces of lead so that the whole block was fixed tightly. After the 'job' was printed, he reversed the process by placing the letters back in the frame in the correct places. In other words, he would have 'dissed' the type—redistributing each piece of type back into the type case ready to be used next time. Type is set upside down and from left to right. That must be why he said years later that he could read swiftly, even if a page was upside down! Gerald used treadle machines, hence the noise and the rhythm that I remember. The treadle turned a wheel, the rollers took the ink from a circular metal plate, the type would be inked by the rollers, and then each sheet of paper would come up to meet the type. Ink and pressure had to be correct, and the paper in exactly the right position. If more than one colour was involved, the ink had to be cleaned off to provide a new surface. After every print run, the rollers and the plate had to be carefully cleaned ready for the next job.

Today there is resurgence in the old methods of printing, despite computerisation and new technology. The craft of hand printing with individual designs has been revived and the old printing presses are rumbling again in craft centres, garden sheds and perhaps old attics.

Printing featured in Gerald's first job. Before going to university, he went to work as a customer/works liaison clerk at City Engraving in Hull. They made plates for the printing trade, employing 300 people in photo-lithograph reproduction and photoengraving. The company needed to schedule jobs, and Gerald was in the middle of processing deliveries between customers, representatives and the shop floor, and reconciling their demands. When he left to study again, he was responsible for customers' requests for quotations and pricing the department's outputs. Sometimes, he had to take lithograph proofs to the station in Hull or Doncaster, to put them on a train to London. Once, at Doncaster, he gave a shilling to a porter for showing him the parcels office, as he was running to meet a deadline. He would often cycle home for lunch, and then perhaps continue with a printing job that he had on the go at home.

At this time, he got to know a Mr Nicoline, whose name Gerald thought had been adapted from the Italian Nicolini. Mr Nicoline had a small printing works called Newland Printing, and Gerald worked for him on some evenings. Perhaps he had met Mr Nicoline through City Engraving, or had bought type from him. Gerald set type for him, and presumably learned from him. They seemed to have a reciprocal arrangement whereby Gerald would work for him in return for the use of equipment for his own little printing jobs. Gerald made friends wherever he went, and this was no exception. He had saved a charming letter from Mr Nicoline, and they kept in touch by letters and visits long after Gerald had moved to London.

In 1968 when at London University, Gerald returned to City Engraving for a summer job, and they made use of his skills once again. Another summer job, in 1969, has a family connection. He obtained a post as a contact man at Nickeloid Engraving Ltd[1] in Southwark, doing much the same as he had done at City Engraving. He wrote of the pressures of London traffic: 'Getting a block to the Motor Trade Gazette by two hours ago can be damaging to the nervous system.' The family connection was told to me by Cousin Richard in New Zealand, who had noted the name in an earlier version of the family trees. Apparently, the firm was co-founded by James Miller, grandfather of Frances Acey (née Boynett), Cousin Richard's wife. Although James would have gone by 1969 when Gerald worked there, one or two of his sons may still have been there—quite a coincidence.

In 1976, after five years at university in London and two years as a banker, Gerald became a full-time printer. He had one or two other jobs after working for National and Grindlays Bank, but eventually decided to go into business on his own. He began in a small way in Norbury, with the help of his great friend, Vincent Palmer. Vincent had worked at the bank, and Gerald had taken over his corporate cases there. Vincent and his wife Cynthia became close friends with Gerald, and moved in retirement to Bristol, visiting Gerald regularly in Wells. Relaxing holidays were enjoyed at their retreat in France. Back in the 1970s, Vincent had bought an estate agent's in Norbury, and Gerald was offered a room there in return for printing the property details and brochures. He jumped at the chance.

At first he helped out at the estate agency while his own business was growing. He bought a printing machine through *Exchange and Mart* for £115, and printed for a variety of clients, including his musical contacts and City firms through his friends and associates. He even stretched to printing for my Doncaster choir.

As his business grew, he needed larger premises, and in 1980 rented an upper floor at 17 Homer Row, London W1. He even employed people on a casual basis when the work demanded. He ran the business from there until 1987, when he moved to Wells. I am told by Roger that the building at Homer Row has a blue plaque relating to C. S. Lewis, who must have lived there. It was spacious, and after our parents died in the early 1980s, our

[1] Previously the Nickeloid Electrotype Company, and affectionately known as 'Old Nick'.

family piano was delivered there by the kind neighbours in Hull. How it was transported up the stairs I do not know. The piano and the large space it occupied came in very useful for occasional singing lessons and group rehearsals. Gerald printed the stationery for weddings for which he played the organ. He must have advertised his printing services while discussing the musical requirements! He even printed for his old employer, the bank, as he had contacts there. He obtained work from the big firms in London such as Burma Oil, and his choirs and church contacts provided him with work. He built up a reasonable business for a few years. He had a mortgage on his lovely little flat in Gloucester Terrace, bought on the strength of a banker's salary, so he had to work hard. However, hard work was always in his blood. He worked his own hours and was not at anyone's beck and call. On more than one occasion he worked through the night to complete an urgent order. The motorcycle couriers were kept busy delivering the work. He learned more about the technicalities of printing at that time, and was knowledgeable about the printing industry.

Gloucester Terrace, London W2, where Gerald had his flat

I recall his printing some little guides for St Mary's, Lowgate, Hull, rewritten by local historian Edward Ingram, whom we visited at his historic house near Filey. There we met his friend Francis Johnson, the renowned architect and adviser on the restoration of numerous Georgian properties in Yorkshire, especially York. They were bemoaning the fact that they had had another break-in, which for these elderly gentlemen was very distressing. We sympathised and then continued with the job of discussing the printing.

Gerald took a great deal of care with his printing, and had the necessary eye for detail. Work for his musical connections was backed by his vast knowledge of the titles and composers, and most importantly, foreign spellings. Roy Wales, his esteemed friend and conductor of the London Chorale and then the English Concert Singers, recalled a typical episode:

> [Gerald] agreed to compile and print an extensive souvenir programme of a Festival of Scandinavian Music I was directing…. I was so impressed with the meticulous care he took to ensure that the spelling and correct accents were given to the many unusual names of the Swedish, Norwegian, Danish and Finnish composers, and the titles of the works represented in the Festival.

Typically, Gerald would have done his research and made the right contacts, so that he was armed with the details.

Gerald's typing skills were legendary. Normally modest, he once wrote: 'I am the fastest typist I know.' I was told that when he helped out at the estate agent's, the secretaries were in awe of his rapid and accurate typing. I suspect that he learned to type at City Engraving and, having to complete work to deadlines, speed went in his favour. Perhaps his Aunt Catherine tutored him or helped with a suitable manual on touch typing. She certainly taught him shorthand in those early days. If he saw that a skill would help him, he took on the challenge. It served him well in the future, as his translating career required vast amounts of word processing. To watch him swiftly and elegantly caressing the computer keyboard whilst translating from Dutch into English was like watching an artist at work. He was able to cross over from musical keyboard to typing keyboard so easily.

When he went to university, he hired a typewriter for £3 and 10 shillings a month (10 shillings is 50 pence today). It paid for itself, as he typed for other students as well as for himself. The days before personal computers were very different for students. In 1970 he bought a Hermes Ambassador typewriter for £44, delivered. It was heavy and, as Gerald remarked, it just about lived up to its advertisement as being portable!

In 1981, when living in Gloucester Terrace, Gerald typed for Anthony Grey, the Reuter journalist, broadcaster and author who had been detained for 27 months in China from 1967 to 1969, the first international hostage of the modern age. I have no idea how they met, but it could have been through the printing business. Grey's book *Hostage in Peking* was published in 1970, and he wrote other books including novels. After 1970 he became a radio and television broadcaster and publisher.

Wells, Somerset

In addition to his 10 years singing in the cathedral choir, Gerald was part of the Wells musical scene for all the 21 years that he lived there. He moved to Wells from London in 1987 to become a lay choir member, (*Vicar Choral*) of Wells Cathedral. He was seeking a change of direction, and his friend Robin Rees had informed him of a vacancy. Gerald wrote of his audition:

> I dashed to the undercroft of the cathedral, where the auditions were held.... Waiting were the Organist and Master of the Choristers, the Assistant Organist and the Precentor. The sight-reading test was a couple of pages in five flats from Elgar's *The Apostles*. I think I sang one wrong note. Later I learnt that Anthony Crossland always set the same extract for tenor auditionees!

'On duty' at Wells Cathedral, *c.* 1990

Vicars' Close in Spring

For his singing duties, Gerald received a small stipend and accommodation in Vicars' Close. This is said to be the oldest complete street in Europe, in that it is two-sided, none of the houses having been replaced or rebuilt since it was built in 1363. Gerald lived in the top flat at No. 5 Vicars' Close when in the choir: later, after renting a house in Wells for two years, he moved back into the Close to rent No. 10. He loved living there, as he describes in the following article:[1]

VICARS' CLOSE, WELLS
The view from within

Those who come to the cathedral hope that their worship will be enhanced by the music daily performed there. The musicians' lives are made much easier by the fact that they live hard by their place of work. But what is it like to live in a picture postcard street?

I remember clearly the moment I first saw Vicars' Close. In 1987 the then Assistant Organist Christopher Brayne offered to show me where I would be living if successful in my audition for a vacancy as a Vicar Choral. As a Yorkshireman who had long lived in London, I had perhaps—just perhaps—once seen a picture of Wells Cathedral in a book, but nothing had prepared me for this. I stood under the archway and thought, 'Yes. I think I *would* like to pass that audition!'

[1] *Newsletter No. 7*, Friends of Cathedral Music, Diocese of Bath and Wells, April 1995, quoted with permission.

The Vicars Choral, in Vicars' Close, *c.* 1990
Gerald is on the right.

Vicars' Close is nowadays viewed by more people than ever before. Some are to be seen clutching guide books, English or foreign, and can be assumed to be informed accurately if concisely. Others are eager to be enlightened if a passing resident has a couple of minutes to spare and it isn't raining. Still others make highly approximate deductions from what they see, or worse: guesses that are way off beam. An exchange might go like this: 'I suppose it's old people who live here nowadays?' (I quote verbatim.) I bridle. 'Well, *I* live here.' (This was before I reached my half-century.) Then I explain a little of the history of this 14th-century jewel.

I tell them that the houses were built for the Vicars Choral by 1363, that the Vicars Choral still live here, that the gardens were added in about 1400, that there were originally 42 houses but are now only 27 as a result of some being made into double houses, and so on. One also has to explain the proper meaning of the word 'vicar'—a substitute; in our case, substitutes for the prebendaries (canons).

Yet in fact we know surprisingly little about the Close. For example, even the date of 1363 is not certain, for the houses could be as late as 1382, and only very recently has it been shown conclusively that the chimneys are original to the houses (though their tops may well have been added a little later).

The Close's charm lies mainly in the interplay between the regularity that the original builders imposed, and the random inconsistencies that decay and modernisation (I use the word relatively) have brought. The 42 original houses had one room downstairs and one room upstairs, each measuring 13 by 20 feet internally. The regularity of the exterior is asserted by the evenly-spaced chimneys and the coping between the houses, the inconsistencies by all manner of features. To mention just a few: the Georgian windows are of different sizes and in different positions from house to house. Some of them have thick glazing bars (indicating an older window frame), some thin. The doorways too are in different positions from one house to another. Most of the doorways have wooden canopies over, but the brackets of these come in a dozen different designs. The garden walls are a hotchpotch of heights, and some have railings whilst others have none. Much of the glass is old: some panes make delicate bull's eye 'shadows' when the sun shines through onto the walls inside.

Queen Elizabeth's 1592 charter to the College of Vicars Choral allowed the Vicars to marry. Each was then allowed two houses, hence the 15 double houses we see today. In the 18th century came a second drastic remodelling, with the insertion of Georgian windows and doorways. And did all the houses at one time have gateways, only a handful of which remain? Even if they did, the gateways must all have been moved or removed when the double houses came into being, to keep them in line with the newly-sited doorways. Hence prints that show all the gateways *in situ* must be anachronistic, reflecting the artist's view of how he thought the Close looked in the past.

The variations inside the houses are even greater than the external inconsistencies. A chief reason for this is that in 1663 the Vicars received licence from the Bishop to lease for 21 years at small rents 'twelve of the most decayed houses', so for the first time strangers were allowed to inhabit the Close. But they insisted on making alterations. The two rooms of No. 13 that look down the Close date from this time, as does the little passageway from the North Liberty.

As for my own accommodation, the first floor of No. 5, the main room is over 12 feet in height and has an 18th-century feel to it. Recently I chanced to meet in Wells my old history tutor, who told me that the banisters are an example of *chinoiserie* and must therefore also be of that century. He also introduced me to the delightful word 'bratticing', used for the miniature machicolations that run at chest height in the wall plates in the attics of the houses. Recent refixing of a loose floorboard in an attic room showed it to be part of the signboard of a seedsman and nurseryman's shop, and one day I hope to find out where it stood.

Gerald outside 5 Vicars' Close, 1994

Whilst the houses are difficult to keep warm, they do have some advantages over modern ones. The thick masonry acts like a great storage heater, helping to even out sudden fluctuations in the temperature outside. In fact the party walls are over two feet thick, which must have provoked some unparliamentary language when doorways had to be knocked through to make the double houses. Still, the solidity of the walls makes it unlikely that one's singing practice will annoy the neighbours.

GERALD BURTON
Vicar Principal

One other aspect of Gerald's time in Vicars' Close merits a mention. From his sitting-room window at No. 5, a penguin beamed benevolently onto those passing in the street below. (One wonders what interpretation overseas tourists may have put on this.) Penguin later acquired a friend, and together they kept view from Gerald's study window in No. 10, as well as, no doubt, assisting him in his translation work.

The Penguins after rehoming by Robin Rees's daughter Bethan

Many people have been inspired by the music of the cathedral over the centuries, and Gerald was aware of the part he played in the continuity of cathedral worship. His knowledge of church music was vast. His interest in history was satisfied by the majestic cathedral and its associated environment, and he felt proud and honoured to be involved in cathedral life. His fine tenor voice must have added much to the choir. He became Vicar Principal for the final three years of his tenure. He described this role as a kind of shop steward, but I gather he carried it out with skill and diplomacy. Each cathedral has its own rituals, the details of which are passed down, so there is much to learn. His service to the choir was longer than that of most members: many of the younger men were recruited for short periods, and Gerald saw many changes of personnel. Over the years several of his colleagues came from America, and Gerald was lucky enough to be invited to their homes for holidays once they had returned to the USA.

The commitment to the choir was enormous, with only one day off per week during the time the choir was in residence. There could be several services in a day, and with practice sessions there could be no straying from the cathedral environs. I read that annually the boys spent more than 300 hours in rehearsal and a further 250 singing the services, so it would be not much less for the men. Gerald's work as a freelance translator of Dutch into English fitted in well with his cathedral duties. During his tenure, he sang an extensive repertoire of music in the settings of the communion service, the canticles, responses, anthems, hymns and carols, with works by many composers spanning the centuries.

Wells Cathedral Choir, 1992
Gerald is at the back on the right, framed in the arch.

The choir's normal complement was 19 boy choristers and 13 gentlemen. There is also now a girls' choir as in many cathedrals nowadays, the boys and girls attending Wells Cathedral School. Although Gerald described the Vicars Choral as dating back to 1136, there were boy choristers singing at Wells even earlier. As well as the daily singing commitments in the cathedral, there were also radio and television broadcasts, plus tours and recitals. The choir recorded music commercially: some of the CDs include Gerald taking an occasional solo spot. He would inform relatives and friends when he would be appearing on television or singing in a radio broadcast. Some services were recorded for broadcast at a later date, but often they would be live with all the attendant production team and rehearsals. One televised candlelit carol service was later broadcast in France. At least once a year, *Choral Evensong* on BBC Radio 3 is broadcast from Wells Cathedral. Uncle Harry wrote in appreciation of the music that was broadcast, and Gerald saved letters from Graham Watson his old music teacher in Hull, who commented on the quality of the music:

> I never cease to wonder at the amazing capabilities of cathedral choir boys of today, and your Choral Evensong this afternoon confirmed my wonder. What further amazed me was how easy the Wells Cathedral Choir made it all sound, and when I checked the pitch at the end they were absolutely on key!

Anthony Crossland was the Organist and Master of the Choristers for most of Gerald's tenure, followed by Malcolm Archer for the final year.

One of Gerald's early adventures with the choir was the 1987 Eleven Towns Tour of Friesland in Holland. These towns are linked by the famous marathon ice-skating race on the canals, which takes place only when the ice is thick enough over the entire route: 15 times in the last 100 years. Gerald's knowledge of the Netherlands and the Dutch language must have come in useful. The choir sang in all the towns on the route, and was congratulated by the chairman of the Eleven Towns committee for 'finishing the course'. The concerts were very well attended, the audiences showing their appreciation of English cathedral singing by standing ovations. The choir was received in the town halls of all the places visited, including Leeuwarden, Sloten, Stavoren and Hindeloopen. There was also a live radio broadcast.

Wells Cathedral Choir singing for the Pope, Rome, 1989

In 1989 the choir visited Rome and Naples, and was privileged to sing for Pope John Paul II. In 1990 it sang in Brussels, in 1993 France, and in 1991 at the enthronement of the new Bishop of Bath and Wells, the Rt Revd James Thompson. In 1993 Wells Cathedral hosted the annual Royal

Maundy Service, a spectacle of colour, ceremony and music. The choir was joined by the Gentlemen and Children of Her Majesty's Chapel Royal in their magnificent garb of red and gold. Chris (my husband) and I were lucky to have a good vantage point in the cathedral. Gerald later received Maundy coins minted specially for the occasion.

In 1994 the choir tackled a more exotic tour, to Brazil. I am sure they did not mind attending the British Embassy for coffee and visiting the lively cities and beaches of that country. The trip was arranged by the British Council, and involved the City of London Sinfonia. Performances were in magnificent churches in several cities of Brazil, so there was much travelling between the venues. The overall organisation (music copies, the choir of boys and men, plus an organ and robes), must have been a triumph, quite apart from the performance of beautiful music.

On tour with Wells Cathedral Choir, São Paulo, Brazil, 1994

There was a notorious incident at São Paulo Airport. As the plane was taxiing along the runway for take-off, it was discovered that a double bass had been left on the runway and was being wheeled away. Its owner was concerned about his precious instrument, and there was to be a performance in Rio that night. After unsuccessful protests to the cabin staff, the orchestra manager entered the cockpit to complain to the captain. When this produced no response, the whole orchestra plus some of the choir members stood up in the aisles. This got results, as the pilot did a sudden U-turn back to the terminal to collect the double bass, with much admiration from the Brazilians on board. One account described the procedure as a plane's equivalent to a handbrake turn. Arrival at Rio de Janeiro was two hours late, but with all the instruments in one place, the concert went ahead on time. News of the incident reached our national newspapers. As it was December, the concerts consisted of carols ancient and modern, plus a varied repertoire of music showcasing the skills of both the choir and the orchestra.

In 1996 the choir visited the USA, namely Newport, Rhode Island for concerts. They no doubt enjoyed a different environment and appreciated the welcome and generosity of their hosts. Americans admire the English cathedral traditions greatly.

But life moves on. Gerald wrote:

> In spring 1997, wanting more freedom, I left the choir after nearly ten years' service. I was sorry to leave my first-floor flat at 5 Vicars' Close, but after renting a cold, unmodernised house in Wells for two years, I moved back into the Close in 1999. This time I am in No. 10, a large house on three floors.

A tribute stated: 'Gerald's contribution to the choir has been immense and he will be sorely missed.' To mark his leaving, the Vicars Choral sang a concert entitled *In Procession*, when music was sung not only from the West gallery but also from the gallery at clerestory level.

Since 2012, the choir's repertoire has included a new anthem: *I will lift up mine eyes* (Psalm 121), by Philip Moore, sometime Organist at York Minster. The opening page reads:

> Dedicated to Gerald David Burton (1944–2008) by his sister Angela Harris and his brother Roger Burton, to commemorate his musical life and especially the ten years' service (1987–1997) in Wells Cathedral Choir, the last three as Vicar Principal. First performed at Evensong on Monday 21 May 2012 by the Boy Choristers and Vicars Choral of Wells Cathedral … directed by Matthew Owens, Organist and Master of the Choristers, accompanied by Jonathan Vaughn, Assistant Organist.[1]

On 'retiring' from the choir, Gerald was able to devote more time to other musical activities and to his translating career. He joined the cathedral's voluntary choir, which substitutes for the normal choir during holiday periods. He would go with them on their annual singing holiday. By one of those marvellous coincidences, choir member Kath Bristow had attended St Mary's Church, Lowgate in Hull as a student, and knew some of Gerald's friends there. He and Kath also undertook library duties together at the cathedral. Gerald made himself available as a proofreader for the cathedral, and sometimes I would see him dashing to the cathedral office to return an article or to collect one. He loved the cathedral environment, and documented through photographs any alterations and

---

[1] Gerald had directed a setting of Ps. 121 at my wedding to Chris [see page 24].

building work. If he should see any rubbish blowing onto Cathedral Green, he would be in hot pursuit. He played the cathedral organ on occasions, his Vicar Choral duties having precluded this earlier. He was also a piano accompanist for various local groups.

His later years in Wells were enlivened by membership of the Mendip Voices, an amateur group who performed at concerts, weddings and other events. They started as a singing group, but on discovering the instrumental talents of their members, began to incorporate these into their repertoire. They performed music ranging from the early sacred choral tradition to modern jazz, folk and songs from musicals. Gerald sang and played his cello, and occasionally the piano and organ.

With his cello and the Mendip Voices

Musical soirées were a feature of these years. He sang solos at birthday celebrations, and extended his repertoire to include comic songs. Gerald certainly left his mark in Wells, making many friends and enriching lives with his musical skills.

Gerald's ideal choir…
with apologies to the Mendip Voices

Already in this chapter there have been several passing references to Gerald's patronage of pubs. A few miles to the north-east of Wells lies the village of Green Ore, and in that village may be found the Ploughboy Inn. Within that establishment, Gerald was a founder member of the Green Ore Independent Traders Society, known to the cognoscenti as the GITS. In that key role he contributed to many late hours' discussion, setting the world and, in particular, the government, to rights with much humour and good banter. His colleagues shared his interest in *Telegraph* howlers, and indeed those of other organs of the press [see next section]. His keen appreciation of his local hostelry and its fine beers was exemplary.[1]

---

[1] Information supplied by fellow GIT Bryn Davies.

The Ploughboy Inn, Green Ore, Somerset

A way with words

Gerald was a wordsmith, and progressed from reading a dictionary as a child to compiling dictionaries as an experienced linguist. Words and print seemed to be in his blood. He had a great affinity with words, and it is not surprising that he became a linguist. His eyes were drawn to print, but because of his experience as a printer, sometimes he would be working out how something had been printed. He was an avid reader and had an encyclopaedic knowledge. His house was full of books on many subjects, and he answered in the affirmative when someone was bold enough to ask him whether he had read them all. He collected old books, especially when these were connected to the family-tree research. He was keen to keep them in good condition, and acquired some good glass-fronted book cases from the local sale room. He was a Welcomer in the Cathedral Library at Wells, and his colleague Kath Bristow wrote in tribute:

> I found to my delight that I had been rostered alongside Gerald. Friday afternoons every fortnight in the summer were enlivened not only by welcoming visitors … but in learning from Gerald's unique insights and appreciation of the Library. I shall always treasure the memories of the care he took in protecting the precious exhibits and pictures from … damaging sunlight, and yet encouraging visitors to see everything.

Gerald certainly regarded his historic books as objects of beauty, and acquired some wonderful books, written in English, about Holland. These must have been the books travellers used in the 19th century.

His extensive work as a translator from Dutch into English meant that he knew his own language inside out, and monitored its changes. He identified when Americanisms had crossed the Atlantic. What would he have made of the current expression 'going forward' substituted for the English 'in future'? He would point out American usage which had been absorbed by his nearest and dearest; such was his grasp of our changing language.

He loved puns, jokes and word origins. He collected ambiguous headlines, and his letters would contain words and their meanings, misprints and journalistic howlers. The latest newsprint howlers would be displayed on his kitchen table at 10 Vicars' Close. If a misprint existed, he would find it. He exchanged these with friends who shared the same interest and sense of humour. His letters would be accompanied by cartoons cut out of newspapers, as he was keen to share a smile with others. Here are a few examples:

[To a shopkeeper] 'Do you keep stationery?'
'No, I wriggle about a bit.'

He drank so prodigiously that not only were his sorrows drowned, his joys didn't stand an earthly either.

Gerald was also a great fan of the radio. He had grown up in the era of great radio humour, with such programmes as *The Goon Show*, *The Navy Lark*, *Round the Horne* and *Hancock's Half Hour*. He enjoyed the quick wit, puns and innuendos of their stars such as Kenneth Horne, Kenneth Williams, Harry Secombe, Tony Hancock and Richard Murdoch. In 1970 he wrote home about *The Goon Show*, and quoted:

'Have you got the statistics?'
'Yes, very badly.'

He admired the humour of stars such as Charlie Chester, Ted Ray and Arthur Askey, who relied on quick wit. Al Read's radio shows were also on his list of favourites. He enjoyed humour based on the clever use of words, and was always a great giggler. According to one friend, he was a quiet mischief-maker in a choir. He would pass some witty remark and, after the ripple effect, some other member of the choir would perhaps be glared at by the conductor with Gerald looking on with a straight face! Here is more of his humour:

Don't tip the waiters—they're unbalanced as it is.

It is kisstomary to cuss the bride.

My bird is as good as my wand.

Blemish, the official language of Belgium.

One small step for man but a taxi ride for Ronnie Corbett.

Saw the silliest mistake ever in Dad's library book—'Bristol Tpyesetting Company'.

Gerald read voraciously and at speed from an early age. He was an excellent speller. A story our mother used to tell was that on a train journey, a lady engaged him in conversation. It was in the days of individual compartments with long seats the width of the carriage, so you had to sit together. The lady asked Gerald to spell some words. All went well. She tried him with increasingly difficult words and ultimately failed in a valiant attempt to catch him out. His mother, looking on, was astounded at his knowledge, as he was only six years old. Cousin Rob remembered Gerald as a boy, reading a dictionary and informing him that he had reached letter P! Later, Gerald rose to great heights in his translating career [see page 74]. The earlier strategy obviously paid off.

Early in his life, Gerald became interested in church records, and this was followed by his liking for genealogy, and his extensive research into all four family trees. In the early 1970s at St Mary's Church, Lowgate, in Hull, he sought information from the registers, in response to Americans and others who were researching their ancestry. Thus he became skilful at reading old writing. He laboriously annotated these records, making them more accessible. He dictated them onto a small tape recorder, and then typed them out over many months. He transcribed all the records dating from 1766 to 1812: there were 20,000 entries of baptisms and burials. They are deposited at the Beverley Records Office near Hull.

During his years at Wells, Gerald researched several aspects of its cathedral. He also researched the membership of the choir in *Extracts from the Chapter Minutes of Wells Cathedral concerning Choristers by Name*. He must have undertaken painstaking research for this. He also researched the history of certain choristers through court records. His work is lodged in the archives at the cathedral. On a somewhat lighter note:

The trouble with the Garden of Eden wasn't the apple on the tree but the pear on the ground.

He went to the Tate Gallery to see a Turner Exhibition. Everyone sees them differently—you could say: 'He has turnered everyone to his own way.'
[Isaiah 53: 6, with apologies to Handel]

I had a bad meal—one bit of chicken I don't think the chicken even knew it had!

Mother asked the assistant at Field's for cheese.
'It's moved to the other counter.'
'What, by itself?'

If you see somebody who appears to step surefootedly through life, the reason could be that he's a goat.

Gerald wrote an extensive treatise about his observations on the use of the English language. He called it *Cloth Ears: the Destruction of English*, sub-titled *Don't mess with my language*. This was the result of observing the demise, in his eyes, of his beloved language and the involvement of newspapers and the radio in this. The treatise begins:

> Why do I get so worked up about the misuse of English? Well I've spent 60 years learning English, starting on my mother's lap and continuing by reading innumerable books by good writers and countless, for the most part well-written, newspapers. It is therefore understandable that I should object to people flaunting their ignorance or, worse, trying to convince me that they're right or, worse still, propagating the view that one form of English is as good as any other.

He illustrated his point of view by quoting examples that he had noted:

> Writers' disdain for the hyphen is to be deplored. Copy writers are the main culprits, though the first example is from the City Diary in the *Daily Telegraph* (correction in brackets):

> '… My daughter told me the leather seats made her car sick.' (car-sick)

The next example is from a leaflet from the British Library:

> '… Henry VIII was one of the most intelligent and *widely read* British kings.' (widely-read)

He treats some 'rules' of English to a common-sense approach. For instance, he advocates the use of a split infinitive in the following case:

> 'The aim of this growth strategy is to more than double the group's turnover within a few years.'

He also writes at length about the use of comparatives:

> Where a comparative or superlative exists, use it. The photographer Norman Parkinson is quoted as having said 'The camera can be the *most deadly* weapon since the assassin's bullet'. If he did say that, he should have said '… the deadliest'.

Here are a few examples from his collection:

> The story has become *more and more murky*. (murkier)

> British rules of engagement are much *more strict*. (stricter)

> This will limit the market to *more wealthy* investors. (wealthier)

> It will become *more cloudy* from the west. (cloudier)

> It is certainly a *more low-profile* event. (lower-profile)

> The Landmark Trust, a charity set up to restore the *more humble* buildings … (humbler)

> *Bruges*, the *most well preserved* medieval city in Belgium … (best-preserved)

He continues:

> Writers often fall into error when they are using a pair of adjectives, and a comparative form exists for one but not the other:
>
> The *most weak* and vulnerable. (the weakest and most vulnerable)

However, he awards full marks for:

> … you could try festooning your fence with many of the rustliest bags you can find.

Gerald goes on to describe other abuses of our language, the absorption of Americanisms, the pronunciation of the word 'bade'[1], the misuse of some words; there is also a treatise on the inconsistencies of some spellings. There are views on the use of expressions such as 'in so far', singular and plural verbs, singular and plural nouns, 'may' and 'might', accents in words, and interesting detail about our changing language.

The cereal packet copywriters' singular

> I've called it this because it's often seen on cereal packets. Many breakfast cereals are plural: such as Corn Flakes and Shreddies. But the people who write the copy that's printed on the packet treat them as singular when they include a banner that reads: 'Contains no added sugar'!

There is certainly food for thought in Gerald's collection (the above being a literal example...) and his musings on language. I have no idea whether he intended to publish it, but it appears to be the basis of a publication. However, he did have a witty letter published in the *Daily Telegraph* in February 2008:

> Sir, Where have all the comparative and superlative forms of adjectives gone? They used to be much more common—sorry, I mean commoner.

Gerald's main means of earning a living after being a banker and a printer was in translating from Dutch to English. His first degree had been in Dutch, and as early as 1972 he was translating English into Dutch (not, as later, solely Dutch into English). The work was for two fellow students at the London Business School, and was a joint effort with a Dutch girl. She and Gerald managed to crack the most formidable expressions such as 'customs clearance depots', and were paid £3 each for their efforts. From occasional requests for small-scale work Gerald developed his skills. Gradually, in the mid-'80s he gave up his printing business in the face of increasing technology. He wrote:

> The turning point was in 1981 or 1982, when the first personal computers came on the market. On the advice of the proprietor of one of the translation agencies I worked for, I bought an Osborne computer, with an Olivetti electronic typewriter as the printer. This package cost

---

[1] This past tense of the verb 'bid' is traditionally pronounced 'bad', *not* 'bayd'.

around £600, but more or less doubled my translating output (and hence my income from it) overnight. The Osborne was advertised as being portable, and it was—just. The integral screen was tiny, about 6 inches by 4, and I worked at it for six months before connecting up the optional 12-inch monitor. The machine had two floppy-disk drives, one with the word-processing package on it and the other for the text files that one created. It could store about 60,000 words in its one megabyte of storage. To put that into perspective, the computer I bought in 1997—my third— has around 2 gigabytes (2000 megabytes) of hard-disk memory, and the fourth, bought in 2003, has 55 gigabytes.

The next technological breakthrough came in the mid-1980s with the arrival of affordable fax machines. Until then, I was in the habit of dashing around central London collecting and delivering translations, or using the motorcycle couriers who appeared in great numbers on the streets of London at around that time. I did not buy a fax machine until I moved to Somerset: it enabled me to leave London without losing my customers there.

He honed his translating skills, as his love of learning and liking for detail led him to an interesting career. He built his client base in Holland by registering with agencies. He translated for more than 35 years. It was an ideal career when singing at Wells: without the time constraints of a regular job, between his choir commitments he could translate at home via his computer. He translated on his first computer at 5 Vicars' Close, and after his move to No. 10 would be hard at work in his compact office overlooking the Close.

Gerald was the first person I knew to own a computer, and it was ideal for his career. At first when he lived in London, his translations were typed, and delivered by fax, post, or courier, but with the advent of email his work went straight down the line! He often used dictation to translate from the Dutch; then he would type from the audio tape, as this was quicker than translating directly onto the computer. He developed good relations with the Dutch agencies with which he worked, and they respected his skill and reliability. When work was required quickly, he would translate into the small hours—though never for more than three or four hours at a time, because of the concentration involved. Some assignments were easier than others: he disliked work in which the original was badly written.

Being a translator is an interesting job, as knowledge of many different subjects is needed. Specialist fields had to be mastered, which he enjoyed, given his wide interests and thirst for knowledge. He had to learn about the Dutch legal system, because much of what he translated had a legal context. It could be a stolen bicycle in Amsterdam, or a dispute over insurance when a warehouse full of margarine had gone up in smoke. The nature of legal work meant that it had to be accurate, and he once told me how responsible he always felt.

However, Gerald could turn his hand to any subject. He translated a book on flower arranging, which took a long time, and he was rewarded by having his name printed as Blurton in the acknowledgement, much to his annoyance! As he needed to embrace the language of flowers and flower arranging, he asked gardeners and flower arrangers for advice. He knew where specialist knowledge might be amongst his friends—his unpaid consultants. Any subject could land on his desk: medical, legal, educational, engineering, and other 'languages' were often checked out with his friends around the country. He sometimes translated for Adrian, Cousin Susan's husband, who had dealings with the Netherlands concerning his mushroom firm; so Gerald learned about mushroom growing. Another relative, Neil, son of Gerald's cousin Jim, also embarked on a translating career, but in different languages, and was grateful for the advice received from Gerald.

Gerald's vast experience in translating led him to write *Powering Past the Pinch Points* (Dutch into English Translating). Inside the front cover of this 165-page book it says:

> Advanced tips for professional translators of Dutch into English. The fruit of 25 years' experience as a commercial translator. How to avoid Dutchisms.

This was published in 2009 by Gateway, the translation agency run by his great friend Aart van den End, with whom he had a very productive working relationship. Sadly, Gerald did not see the book in its final form. It is a resource for the use of translators and those studying translating, and is suited to the types of translation involving legal, property and commercial issues, as well as other subjects. In it he shares the knowledge that he had accrued over many years, and although I can only read the English parts, I can appreciate the detail that is included. The Dutch recipients have declared that it is an excellent resource. One wrote: 'I found it a jewel, just what I needed. It contains everything that I come across in the texts that I translate. I am very enthusiastic about this publication.' This was from a translator and secretary in a law firm in Rotterdam. There were many words of praise for his efforts from students and translators. This is a great legacy, and I am proud to own a copy.

Gerald translated for agencies and firms in the Netherlands and in Britain, and as he built his reputation, so friendships were made. He was very well regarded in the translation world. Sometimes he had more work than he could manage, and he would put up his prices to discourage work. However, the ploy failed, as his customers always came back to him. As he was self-employed, he had all the additional tasks of running a business. He administered the business himself, with one of his ex-choir colleagues Rob Rüütel processing the invoices and payments.

Gerald worked for a few years with Aart van den End in compiling specialist dictionaries. These were the *Onroerend Goed Lexicon* (The Property

Lexicon, 1999) and the *Juridisch Lexicon* (The Legal Lexicon, 2005). Aart and Gerald spent many hours on the phone while this work progressed, discussing the finer points of word meanings, as cultural, legal and technical differences between the two nations would be brought into play. There was not always an equivalent expression, but one had to be found! Aart and Netty, his wife, were supportive of Gerald in his last weeks, visiting Wells to see him. They had one of those valuable friendships whereby lives were enriched through shared interests. Aart wrote:

> Gerald was a very special and highly-valued member of the Gateway 'family'. From the very moment that Gateway was founded in the early 1980s, Aart and Gerald recognised in each other a true language professional. They were also friends and 'brothers in arms' in all aspects of language and translation. Music was also a shared passion. So much so, that they even took to listening together to the bell-ringers of Wells Cathedral, figuring out the system of change-ringing. Gerald and Aart spent a great deal of time together, sometimes in each other's company at Aart's office in Zeist or at Gerald's ... 14th-century house in Wells, but usually several times a day on the telephone. He made a regular contribution to the Lexicons and is rightly mentioned in each foreword.

One of Gerald's fellow translators, Judith Wilkinson, wrote of him:

> I met Gerald in London in a choir ... over 20 years ago. I was just starting out as a translator, working from Dutch into English. Gerald was already a seasoned translator ... and he invited me to his office, where he gave me a great deal of invaluable advice. I also caught a glimpse of him at work, and I remember being astounded at the speed with which he could produce a text; the translation would fly onto the page as if by magic. He immediately—and with characteristic generosity—offered me some work: he was in the middle of translating a book on Indonesian cookery and was happy to share the job. (Years later he said that it had been one of the few jobs that had caused him nightmares, as he worried that he might have got the quantities of chilli powder wrong.)
>
> Over the years we became friends and colleagues. We worked for some of the same clients, and would occasionally share translation assignments. When Gerald moved to Wells, we stayed in contact and continued to collaborate from time to time. Gerald was the best translator I ever met, and I picked his brains far more than he picked mine. He was always cheerful and chatty on the phone, always made time for my queries, and was simply a mine of information on the most unlikely topics.... I will miss his friendship, his good humour and his expertise.

3

When Words Leave Off

When words leave off, music begins.

Heinrich Heine

Early musical days

To say that we came from a musical family is perhaps an exaggeration, but we became one. There must have been models somewhere. The previous two generations played the piano and sang, in the days when many houses had a piano. Our maternal grandfather Frank Barnes played the piano quite well; our father played too, and we all had piano lessons. The amateurs of the previous generation produced singers, instrumentalists, music teachers and a violin maker. Many instruments were mastered amongst the 15 Barnes cousins, and singsongs round the piano featured in our Christmases. We were a churchgoing family, and many of the cousins sang in church choirs, at least as children.

Gerald's music teacher in the first class at Newland C. of E. School, Hull, was Mrs Mitchell, a leading light in local folk dancing. (Her husband later taught Gerald at Hymers College.) Initially he played those percussion instruments for small hands, used in early singing games and songs. He began piano lessons with Miss Phyllis Futty, who placed a penny on the back of the hand; Gerald once declared that she put flour on her face instead of powder. With parental backing he mastered the piano early on, and began organ lessons at Hymers College with Graham Watson, for many years organist at St Mary's, Beverley. Gerald maintained a lifelong friendship with him and his wife. Gerald's other organ and theory teachers were Ronald Styles (a teacher at Hymers College) from Holy Trinity in Hull, and Albert Hall [*sic*], also known as Bert Hall, from St Mary's, Lowgate. Gerald often practised the organ at St Mary's, Beverley, where Graham Watson taught him. Many years later I found a charming recording of them discussing the St Mary's organ, and reminiscing about the Hymers staff. Gerald frequently carried a small tape recorder, and had a valuable habit of recording conversations, usually with prior permission but on rare occasions with retrospective agreement!

Gerald became a choirboy at St Mary's, Lowgate, Hull, at the age of eight or nine. His mother had encouraged him, and he joked that he joined the choir because he thought the seats would be more comfortable! This experience provided his grounding in church music and rituals, supplemented by his membership of the Servers' Guild. He was involved in church music for the rest of his life. Although he stayed in Hull only until his early 20s, Gerald never ceased to support St Mary's, calling it his spiritual home. He began bell-ringing, but as the tower of St Mary's was deemed unsafe in those days, the bells were rung from a primitive keyboard set-up in the tower, and later all bell-ringing ceased for many years. Today, after the church's restoration, they can be played in the proper manner.

As a choirboy, 1955

Gerald joined the Lowgate Choral Society, and was on the church's music committee. He acted in a drama group called The Company of the Way, and one of his roles was as an angel. The lunchtime concerts at the church became a feature of Hull city life.

At school, Gerald was drawn into choirs and orchestras. As well as piano and organ lessons, he learned to play the cello. Whenever I hear the Polka from *Schwanda the Bagpiper* by Weinberger, it brings back fond memories of a school concert, with Gerald playing a cello nearly as big as himself. He must have looked back in gratitude to the teachers who nurtured his talents during those early years.

In 1960, a transaction took place regarding a cello which was wasting its life hanging in a barn in Skeffling, a village in the eastern reaches of East Yorkshire. Cousin Rob Barnes informed Gerald that the 'Skeffling cello', as it became known, was populated with woodworm. Rob wrote:

> Together with a restorer called Mr Burgan, who lived in Beverley, we[1] took it apart and put it together again. I remember boiling up a mixture of rosin and beeswax to fill the woodworm holes in the neck of the instrument. It was slightly smaller than a normal cello, much repaired, with a badly fixed crack on the front. I dare say somebody eventually repaired it properly. If it had been hanging in a barn in Skeffling, it was most likely used by a pre-Victorian village band, possibly for church services. From the late 1880s churches tended to install organs, and the village players were no longer needed.

Gerald bought the cello for 10 shillings from a farmer called John Ward, and brought it back to Hull on one of the famous old Connor and Graham buses, which rattled over that flat landscape. He thought that a relative of John Ward had once played the cello at the New Theatre in Hull. The Skeffling cello was sold to Cousin Rob, who made further use of it.

Choirs and more

There is much more to singing than being involved in a choir. Gerald had sung in choirs for most of his formative years, at school and at church. He sought choirs in all the places where he studied and worked. Exercising his fine lyric tenor voice in choirs was the origin of many friendships, and was a reason to travel. Music, especially in this form, is a great social engine, opening doors to talented teachers and conductors, renowned concert halls, majestic places of worship, and wonderful and varied music. Travel was high on Gerald's list of delights, and his singing experiences took him to many countries, as well as extending his knowledge of Britain. Already a gifted linguist specialising in Dutch, he could speak some other languages, but would make the effort to learn another one if the trip demanded it. He sang a vast range of music, from the great choral works to folk songs and the musicals, pieces modern and ancient, well-known and rare, and by composers of many different eras and nationalities. He performed in all the major concert halls in London, and in cathedrals, churches, theatres and other venues in this country and abroad. No wonder he once strayed from his normal modesty to write that he had probably sung more music than anyone of his quality of voice. Occasionally choirs would recruit him for particular performances, as he was experienced and reliable.

---

[1] Presumably Rob and Gerald.

In the early 1970s, Gerald joined the London Chorale, formed in 1963 by the celebrated conductor Dr Roy Wales, who directed it for 17 years. This prolific and prizewinning choir performed in many venues, including the Royal Albert Hall, Barbican, Royal Festival Hall, Queen Elizabeth Hall, Purcell Room, St John's Smith Square, St Mary's Bryanston Square, Fairfield Halls Croydon, and Midlands venues where Roy had been based. Trips abroad meant that the choir graced many a foreign stage or place of worship. It was a busy time: in 1976 Gerald wrote that there were 28 rehearsals and five performances in less than 10 weeks!

There were many premieres of works by contemporary composers and several commercial recordings:

> The London Chorale keeps me fairly busy … most of the choir are singing in a concert at the Purcell Room next Saturday. The music is by one composer, Stephen Dodgson; he came to last Wednesday's rehearsal, so of course it was tremendously hard work, as we didn't want to disappoint him with our progress.

A month later there were rehearsals for a first British performance:

> We've now started learning Bernstein's Mass, to be performed with the Birmingham Symphony Orchestra at the Coventry Theatre on 16 May, and the following day at the Royal Albert Hall. The vocal score is enormous—in fact when I saw an instruction in the text for the priest to ascend the steps as if carrying a heavy burden (the work is acted as well as sung), I suggested somebody must have given him the full score to carry!

After four rehearsals in six days, it was off to Warwick to rehearse on Friday and Saturday for the performance on Sunday, only meeting the orchestra for the first time on the Sunday afternoon:

> There were about 1500 people there for the performance in the evening, even if the poster outside was still advertising Danny La Rue—somebody claimed to have found one of his sequins on the stage! The lighting was chaotic, as the *Birmingham Post* reported next morning. On Monday 17th we turned up at the Royal Albert Hall … waiting patiently as Roy was busy getting his pound of flesh out of the expensive orchestra.… We were a little awed by the sight of people everywhere, and all arriving for our little show! The place seemed about three-quarters full, with perhaps 5000 people, so I don't think Roy would have had trouble getting money at the box office. Later we even got £3 a head towards our expenses. Everything went well, and it must have looked impressive to see the main chorus of around 120, a street choir of 40, Southend Boys' Choir (about 30), the orchestra (part on stage as the Street Band), the rock group, the dancers and the soloists, all moving as prescribed. In particular, we in the street choir had, for instance, a complicated marching sequence and a 'fetishistic dance' lasting about five minutes, as well as lots of other movement.…

The reviewers were quite keen on the Albert Hall performance … the *Financial Times* critic didn't like the music as such, but apart from an ungrateful remark about the dancers, he couldn't think of anything much to say against our performance.

Madeleine Acey, Cousin Richard's daughter, recalls meeting Bernstein:

When I was around four years old, Dad was working for a record company, Phonogram, in Wellington. Leonard Bernstein was coming to New Zealand, and Dad was horrified to discover that no one from the record company (or anywhere else) was due to meet him at the airport. So we went to meet him. I remember being there with my parents, and Bernstein was loud and exuberant and wearing a Black Watch tartan suit! He kissed me on the cheek, and I remember his stubble.

1976 also found Gerald with the London Chorale in Amsterdam. They indulged in eating and drinking at unsocial hours, but managed to sing in a concert, and with 'the indispensable aid of a clock's piercing alarm', to make a live recording in the Van Gogh Museum.

After a brief microphone rehearsal and an ordinary rehearsal which hardly lasted much longer, we went on at 12.25 p.m., singing three items: *Where the Bee Sucks* (Arne), one of Antonín Tučapský's new madrigals, of which we gave the first performance only the other week at St John's Smith Square, and a Negro spiritual, *Ain't Got Time to Die*—a wide range, as usual when the Chorale sings!

Singing in the Chorale was hard work. Gerald recorded that 12 of them had learned 14 songs in six rehearsals for a concert at St Mary's Bryanston Square, repeated in Oxfordshire the same week. There were songs by Finzi, Vaughan Williams, Holst and Milford. On another occasion they performed *Russian Songs for Men*. If variety is the spice of life, they certainly had it in quantity. The Royal Albert Hall saw them in a Viennese Evening conducted by Vilem Tausky. Other famous conductors had them under their batons, most notably Marcus Dods. I once went to the Queen Elizabeth Hall to hear Gerald sing in Orff's *Carmina Burana*. I ended up on the front row, as some extra seats had been inserted. This was fine except that I shot out of my seat every now and then, as I was next to the percussion section! However, I could see the choir and Gerald very well.

I know only of some performances, but there were many more. Gerald wrote to Roy Wales after the latter's temporary move to Australia:

Then it was straight to Ightham Mote, near Sevenoaks. There the National Trust were raising money to do up this beautiful moated manor house, and 700 people turned up, mostly dressed as if for Glyndebourne, paying £7 a ticket (this was 1986) and bearing their rugs, cool boxes of champagne, candelabra … to sit on the big lawn and listen to *us*, the Chorale. We sang for two 45-minute sessions, efficient stage lighting having been rigged up for later, and it was just great. I think the Chorale got £400; it was sponsored by Johnson's Wax, and the Johnson's man was so impressed he told the Chorale committee we could write a blank cheque for next year for our costs.

As well as showing their skills in the great classical choral works, which they performed in a range of venues, there were the big concerts such as the Classic Spectaculars promoted by Raymond Gubbay, in venues including the Royal Albert and Queen Elizabeth Halls. These were popular concerts, which must have been money spinners. The Chorale also graced the Ritz Hotel with Christmas carols.

Singing with the London Chorale
Gerald is at the back, second from the left.

They took part in competitions and invariably won prizes. Every couple of years, they would compete in an eisteddfod. One year, Gerald recorded: 'We won the mixed choir class and our girls won their class, and as the prize money is not insignificant, it is a useful addition to the choir's hard-pressed funds.' They took part in the BBC *Let the Peoples Sing* competition. It was recorded in the Concert Hall of Broadcasting House, and he once asked our parents if they wanted to watch the recording session. One year, the Chorale beat Schola Cantorum of Oxford in the contemporary class. They also competed in Blackpool, Italy and Belgium. Prague saw them compete with choirs from Berlin, Moscow and Budapest. They also participated in a Festival of Choirs in the Royal Albert Hall.

One year they competed in Montreux, with their new conductor David Coleman. I went along, as I considered it was the only way I would get to see Switzerland. It was great fun, and the side trips added to the experience.

That was probably the trip when Gerald managed to get all the way to Switzerland with an old passport, as he had had a break-in at his flat, and realised too late that his passport had been taken. It was all plain sailing until he tried to get back into Britain, when he had some explaining to do!

Gerald went to America with the Chorale in 1986. He wrote about:

> … sightseeing experiences that hardly anyone wanted to miss out on in New York, like going to the top of the World Trade Centre of course and taking the Staten Island ferry—a chilly business standing on the foredeck to photograph the skyline and the Statue of Liberty, now with its scaffolding removed. The lunchtime concert at Holy Trinity, Wall Street, was attended by about 500 people, to our great surprise—this is quite normal. I think it made some of our singers quite nervous. Equally enjoyable was the concert in the foyer of the UN Building. Some of us took a cab to Greenwich Village in search of food. We described to the driver all the places we'd been to on the tour, and explained that New York was the last place. 'Yeah', he said, after reflecting for a moment, 'you did right. You wouldn't have wanted to do the trip the other way round, starting off here and then going to all them other … !' Obviously he didn't rate anywhere outside New York. Well, I *did* like all the other places.

Further trips took Gerald to far-flung places with the Chorale and, later, with the English Concert Singers. When Roy Wales returned from Australia in the late '80s, he formed the English Concert Singers and the English Concert Chorus (a somewhat extended group). Gerald joined them, sometimes as a soloist, whenever his duties at the cathedral permitted. Later, in 1999, one notable tour involved the Singers in a busy schedule on the east coast of Australia: Sydney, Brisbane, the Gold Coast, Mackay and Cairns. They sang at Christ Church St Lawrence in Sydney, before travelling up the coast to Brisbane by train. I understand they had to draw lots for the most comfortable places on board, and Gerald was lucky to get good sleeper accommodation on this long trip. In Brisbane they performed at the Queensland Conservatorium of Music, where Roy had been Director. Free time in Australia was exciting. For example, after a helicopter ride and catamaran trip to the Great Barrier Reef, Gerald wrote: 'We saw scores of kinds of beautiful fish, with unbelievable colours and patterns.'[1] This was followed by a concert in St Monica's Cathedral in Cairns. On that trip Gerald met with John and Jo Fauvet, London Chorale friends living in Sydney. Such is the close fraternity of choirs that they meet on the other side of the world.

---

[1] My husband Chris and I took a similar trip in recent years, but by car, and experienced the scenic train ride from Cairns to Kuranda in the rain forest, then back by the Sky Rail, the long and exhilarating ride by cable car over the tree tops that Gerald had described some 11 years earlier.

In 2006, on my second trip Down Under with Gerald, we met John and his daughter, Francesca. After a meal near the Sydney Opera House, we attended a fine performance of *Madama Butterfly*. When we took a breather outside at the interval, Gerald commented that the recent scene on the stage could have been enacted outside. He was quite right: the aura of Sydney Harbour with the moon shining was remarkably similar to the moonlit stage setting that we had witnessed moments before. That was a truly memorable evening.

On Gerald's foreign trips, the side tours added to the experience, whether it was nervously holding a koala, balancing on a camel in Tangiers, being photographed with the famous apes at the Rock of Gibraltar, or sampling the real Guinness in an Irish pub.

On a camel, Tangiers, 1998

In addition to *Let the Peoples Sing*, other radio broadcasts were a feature of Chorale life. In 1981 Gerald gave an interview about the Chorale on Belgian radio, arranged by his friend Chris Coggill, then living in Brussels.

He wrote in a letter to our mother:

> I'd already typed out a script before I left London. The format was about 20 minutes of music and 10 minutes of talking about the London Chorale. As this was for the French side of Belgian radio, the original plan of doing it in Dutch was thrown out of the window. As my French isn't up to replying to questions, although the questions were in French and I could more or less understand … my replies were in English, and the interviewer translated into French for the benefit of the listeners. The programme went out the same evening, as I was on my way back to Heathrow. I chose extracts from the recordings of music by Paul Patterson and Antonín Tučapský that the Chorale had made. The programme was one of a series called *Mille et Une Voix* (a thousand and one voices). The interviewer wasn't able to find out until we were half-way through just how many minutes were to be filled, but we were only a minute over the required length, so it was a question of fading out the last piece of music.

As always, Gerald rose to the challenge of a new experience.

After the exhilaration of singing in a concert, the inevitable post-concert celebrations and late-night cabarets aided the winding-down. Gerald often featured in the cabarets. There were set pieces, duets and take-offs, and I found a photograph of Gerald dressed as Hinge (or was it Bracket?) complete with wig.[1] Choir members would improvise when abroad, and the performance would reflect their environment with whatever props were available. A great deal of jollity ensued. There were occasions when they would burst into song in airports, in hotels or on station platforms, much to the amusement of any transient audience.

There were many fine first performances of works by composers such as Paul Patterson and Antonín Tučapský, who were thrilled at the Chorale and its successors [see page 85] showcasing their work so ably. They have performed extensively both here and abroad. It seemed that the venues were very much related to the part of the country where Roy Wales lived and worked, as the focus moved from the Midlands to Sussex in the latter years. Roy would invite Gerald to sing in concerts, including on one occasion in Guernsey. Gerald printed for his musical contacts, including programmes and other material for the London Chorale when he had his printing business in London. He was always pleased to be involved with Roy Wales's ventures, and enjoyed all aspects of choral life. It made him very busy. He wrote: 'Last night the Chorale had a big concert at the Queen Elizabeth Hall, so I was very busy with rehearsals and printing the programmes.'

---

[1] Dr Evadne Hinge and Dame Hilda Bracket were fictional 'mature' ladies, played by men in drag. Their act, which was based on their supposed musical careers in their younger days, appeared first in cabaret, and later on radio and television, for 30 years.

The Grove Singers (probably the only choir named after a pub) was formed from the remnants of the Chorale. They sometimes invited Gerald to sing, in the choir or as a soloist. He toured Northern Italy with them and sang High Mass in St Mark's, Venice. Other choirs near Wells also asked him to sing with them. He was a valued member, being reliable and having a fine voice. He relished the challenges of new works, but also enjoyed performing music that he had sung many times.

The St Hugh Singers

For almost 30 years, the St Hugh Singers provided another outlet for Gerald's musical talents. A chance meeting on Ealing Broadway station in 1968 started it all. Gerald knew Robin Rees by sight at Bedford College, and one day the two of them entered into conversation. Thus, a 40-year friendship began. At the time both were commuting from Ealing, and Robin suggested that Gerald join Bedford College Choir, which he conducted.

Subsequently they founded the St Hugh Singers from former participants on the Royal School of Church Music (RSCM) summer course at Lincoln Cathedral. Robin had encouraged Gerald to attend the 1975 course. The plan for the choir was hatched in 1977 by Gerald and Robin, by then Lincoln 'regulars'. They were joint administrators from 1979 to 2006, and spent many an hour on the phone discussing the choir's endeavours.

The name St Hugh Singers was adopted because of Hugh's involvement in the building of the Angel Choir in Lincoln Cathedral. St Hugh of Avalon, a Frenchman, set about rebuilding the cathedral after its destruction by an earthquake in 1185, and he really did take part in the work. The hod with which he was believed to have carried bricks became a sacred object at his shrine after his death. The superb Angel Choir was built as a memorial to St Hugh, and cures were reputed to have taken place at his shrine. While living in Wells, Gerald discovered that the East Somerset Railway used to run through Wells to Witham where, 800 years earlier, St Hugh had been the Prior.

The RSCM courses at Lincoln had no age barrier for tenors and basses, but an upper age limit of 21 for sopranos and altos. I now understand the attraction! The St Hugh Singers had no such rule. The purpose of the group was to sing a weekend of services in cathedrals and collegiate chapels once or twice a year during the break by the usual choir. Their singing odyssey reached 34 venues over the years, including Canterbury, Durham, Ely, Exeter, Lincoln, Salisbury, St Albans, and Winchester Cathedrals, and Beverley and York Minsters. Some venues were revisited on one or more occasions. They even substituted at Wells Cathedral in the spring of 1998, after Gerald had left his post in the choir there.

Some 30 singers volunteered for the first weekend at Guildford, and a choir of around 40 regular members soon grew up. Friendships were forged in the St Hugh 'family' through the Christian music-making, and no doubt during the socialising afterwards.

The detailed organisation was in good hands. For each weekend gathering, a specialist church musician was invited as director, and the director appointed an organist. As each cathedral has its own traditions and customs, intricate details had to be mastered, and I understand that the organisation was not always straightforward. Robin and Gerald had to be quick learners and ask the right questions. Advance planning of venues, music, accommodation and finances all took time and patience. The singers came together from all parts of Britain, and had to be skilled and familiar with the music, as there was precious little time to rehearse. Having females in the group must have been a new experience for some cathedrals in the early years, before girl choirs were established.

The St Hugh Singers, Guildford Cathedral, 1984
Gerald is second from left on the back row,
with Robin Rees in front to Gerald's left.

The singing was not confined to places of worship, such was their enthusiasm. I suspect it happened with the St Hugh Singers, but on at least one occasion, (according to one of Gerald's letters) after the RSCM course at Lincoln, some of the group 'sang on the platform at Lincoln station, in the guard's van and a little in the mainline train. The other passengers were quite amused.'

Gerald and Robin made a strong team, and were valued for their musicianship, patience and commitment to the group. They laid a great foundation for a group of church musicians which met for a final time in 2014—at Lincoln.

Adventures in organ playing

Gerald played church organs for all of his adult life, and it was only his singing duties at Wells Cathedral that prevented him from playing regularly for those 10 years. He transferred his piano-playing skills to the organ in his teenage years, and was taught by several organists in Hull. He had passed his Piano and Music Theory exams, and gained a Distinction in Grade 8 Organ at the age of 21. I learned from Ian Hare, who became a professional organist, that after hearing Gerald's playing at Hymers College, he wished to emulate him. They were both taught by Graham Watson.

Gerald was the organist and choirmaster at St Saviour's, Wilmington in Hull, from the age of 17 to 22, when he left for London, but returned to help out in vacations. At first the vicar there was Father Fox. He was a kindly man who had lost an arm in the First World War, and a choirboy or server would hold his books for him during services. After his retirement to Bournemouth he and Gerald kept in touch by letter. The next vicar was Paul Thieme, a Dutchman, also a musician, who was interested in church music. He instructed the young couples who wished to be married in his church, and he took great delight in regaling the tale of one wedding. After telling the happy couple to follow him to the altar rail, he was horrified on turning to find them progressing forward on their knees. He had omitted to tell them to stand up first, and vowed to be more precise in future.

Sometimes I would go along and help or hinder when Gerald was playing the organ; I would turn the pages or hand him music. On one occasion he said he was playing just for me, and I treasure that occasion. He played other organs in the Hull area, earning money which came in useful for financing lessons and buying music. Such earnings continued for most of his life. He helped out at his old church, St Mary's, Lowgate. At Christmas he would play when the choirmaster, Bert Hall, was conducting the Carol Service. Gerald wrote that once when he was playing at St Mary's, he foolishly 'tried to play the unison arrangement of hymn 544 and got into difficulties'. He must have had the same adventures in the organ loft as any organist, with the wrong hymn, too many or too few verses or a clumsy page turn; it was part and parcel of the job.

On moving to Ealing when he entered London University in the late 1960s, Gerald familiarised himself with the local churches, so that he could find not only an organ to play, but also a church choir of quality. He settled on Ealing Green Congregational (later Ealing Green Church), where he was subsequently welcomed as the organist and choirmaster. He attended courses for choirmasters at the Royal School of Church Music's headquarters (then at Addington Palace, Croydon), to equip him for the task. Although brought up in the high Church of England tradition, Gerald was attracted to this church after practising the organ there. He commented in a letter home: 'They have a nice well-balanced choir.' He earned £1 for every week that he played, supplementing his student grant. As well as the regular services, there were extra fees for weddings and funerals (£2 for a wedding in 1970). Once he wrote: 'I got to choir on Friday to find that I was taking the practice and nobody had told me!' However, he must have been well received as he wrote later that the previous incumbent had said one Sunday that 'I had played splendidly this morning!' At about this time, the church notes stated: 'We offer our special thanks to Gerald Burton for so ably playing for this service which the organist is least likely to enjoy' (the Christmas service).

The Ealing congregation soon took Gerald under its wing, and apparently he was never short of a Sunday lunch from then on. He would enjoy their hospitality on Sunday afternoons before returning to play for the evening service. He made lifelong friends there, and joined in the church and community activities, including helping the minister's wife in the War on Want charity shop. He said it was one of the most profitable shops and they had great fun. There were also variety shows to raise money for church funds, and Gerald provided the piano accompaniment to the cabaret items, which invariably involved men dressing up as women. A rendition of *Oh No John, No John* was remarked upon. One of his Ealing friends later followed him to the West Country after training for the ministry, and the friendship was renewed. Gerald was able to borrow one of his friend's dog collars for a show that he was in.

Gerald was well regarded in Ealing, and ran the choir skilfully. He wrote home: 'A lot of people said they had enjoyed my playing. Fortunately I had been able to get several hours of practice in during the week.' Bert Hall, his teacher and mentor in Hull, had once written reminding him that a choirmaster should always be in charge!

He practised the organ at the Royal College of Organists at this time, and wrote of playing the Chaplin practice organ there. He said it had two manuals (keyboards), six stops and no swell pedal which: 'simplifies the Hindemith considerably'. There were more harmony and organ lessons at that period.

In 1971 Gerald attended the Royal College of Organists Dinner at the Savoy Hotel. He relates: 'I just happened to mention it in passing to one of the choir members, and the next I know is that the church deacons are offering to buy me a ticket'. He was accompanied to this grand event by Celia Fairbrother, one of his university friends, who recalled many years later what a superb experience it had been. Gerald wrote home, suitably impressed by the main speaker, who happened to be the Prime Minister at the time: Edward Heath, organist and sometime organ scholar at Balliol College, Oxford:

Everything went off perfectly at the dinner.... There were some 410 guests, about 10 to each round table, apart from the top table where the high-ups sat.… Ted Heath made a long and amusing speech; the president Dr William Cole announced in his speech that Herbert Howells, whom I caught sight of there, had just completed his *magnum opus* for organ. Apparently, years ago when Howells and the Prime Minister met, Howells said that he would one day write an organ work far exceeding in scope anything he had composed for the instrument hitherto, and that he would dedicate it to Heath if the latter had become Prime Minister by then—and so it has turned out. At the end of the dinner (magnificent food, of course), it was announced that the Parlour Bar would be open, so Celia and I located it, and found that the P.M. was already there; if we'd been a little bolder straight away, we could have had a chat with him.… We edged closer to him later, however, and both got our menus signed; he said a few 'Goodnight's to those of us who were nearest to him when he left (preceded by a man who looked like his bodyguard). He is a nicer man than I previously thought, and that seemed to be the reaction of the students who met him here[1] last term.

The Prime Minister said choosing your colleagues in government was rather like choosing the stops on an organ—but sometimes one needed to change the registration—obviously a reference to an impending reshuffle! Big organ names at the dinner included: Francis Jackson (York), John Birch, Herrick Bunney (Edinburgh), Lionel Dakers, Dr Harold Darke (one of the few I knew by sight), Sir John Dykes Bower (formerly St Paul's), Douglas Guest (Westminster Abbey), Douglas Hawkridge, Lady Jeans, Professor Keys (Professor of Music at Nottingham and then Birmingham—I heard him say in the Parlour Bar afterwards: 'It's like musicology: you've got to go to the original source— this is where they serve the drinks'). Other celebrities included: Noel Mander (the organ builder), Martin Neary (Winchester), Dr Arthur Pritchard, Noel Rawsthorne (Liverpool), Bernard Rose (Magdalen College, Oxford), Martindale Sidwell (St Clement Danes), Herbert Sumsion (formerly Gloucester), Alwyn Surplice (Winchester), Eric Thiman (City Temple), Robert Vincent (formerly Hull), Sir Jack Westrup, David Williams, Dr Arthur Wills (Ely). Apologies were conveyed from Sir William McKie (formerly Westminster Abbey) and George Thalben-Ball (Temple Church), who to our great amusement, was practising in Westminster Abbey for a recital there the following day—of course with all the thousands of visitors in there during the day, it's the only time he could fit his practice in!

Many of these names are familiar as composers of church music. After reading Gerald's full account of the dinner, our mother responded: 'I enjoyed reading about the dinner.… I galloped up the stairs two at a time', such was her excitement.

[1] The London Business School.

From the mid-1970s, Gerald played for services at many London churches, and in the chapels of St Mary's Hospital, Paddington, near his flat in Gloucester Terrace, and the Middlesex Hospital. (Years earlier he had played for services at the Children's Hospital in Hull.) One morning at St Mary's, nobody turned up. About 15 minutes after the service should have started, a fireman came in, wanting to look out of the window to see where some smoke was coming from! There had been a fire at 7.30 a.m., causing quite a bit of damage. Gerald could smell smoke in the chapel, so that explained why the service was not taking place!

Playing the new Flentrop organ, Dunblane Cathedral, 1992

At all the other churches where he played, he seemed to deputise and did not have a permanent post. But then, with all his other musical activities, this arrangement suited him as he could pick and choose when he played. He played for weddings, funerals and regular services at Kensal Green Church, St Mary's Bryanston Square (where he also sang in the choir), Christ Church Albany Street, St John's Hoxton, Westbourne Park Baptist Church, Kensington Chapel, St John's Harrow Road—and many more. He must have had a great time playing all the different instruments. He played organs wherever he was in the world, with permission. He once found an organ to play in Stuttgart, and on a visit to choir friends Bill and Mary Craig, they photographed him playing Dunblane Cathedral's new Flentrop organ. He still played at Ealing Green as a stand-in, as he was always willing to help out. A very patient teacher, he also gave organ lessons to friends.

On several occasions Gerald was asked by family and friends to play at weddings. He played at Sewerby Church near Bridlington when his cousin Susan married Adrian Dawes. Susan requested the Toccata from Widor's *Fifth Symphony* and, although he had not played it in public before, he did a good job, much to his relief. He had been concerned about playing such a piece on an unfamiliar organ, but he need not have worried, as he would have practised well.

Some years earlier he had travelled with the family in a hire car to play at his cousin Jim's wedding to Cilla in Lincolnshire. He was keen to arrive in time, as there had been no opportunity to familiarise himself with the organ. The estimate of the journey time was faulty, but after some anxious moments all was well and he triumphed yet again on a strange organ. The last time he was asked to play was for the next generation, at the wedding in Sussex of Michelle, younger daughter of Susan and Adrian. This time he did have prior practice. Michelle and groom Anthony appreciated his performance, as did the congregation. Indeed the whole family was, as always, proud of his skills.

After leaving the cathedral choir, Gerald was recruited to play at three village churches near Wells: Ston Easton, Litton and Chewton Mendip. He would go from one to the other in the same morning to play for the services, sometimes taking the vicar along with him. He needed deputies, just as he had deputised in London, and on one occasion recruited a stand-in by literally bumping into someone in the street. Talk about luck! He played the organ for the wedding of Paul Martin of television fame on programmes such as *Flog It*, but having no television, he had no idea who he was. Gerald's death was a big loss to those three churches and their respective communities.

The organ-playing fraternity is a truly international one. In 2006 in Whitianga, on the Coromandel peninsula in New Zealand, Gerald and I climbed aboard a little boat for a scenic trip along the coast to see Cathedral Cove. Who should appear in the final seconds before we sailed but the prolific musician Peter Averi! He and Gerald exchanged organ-playing experiences as the magnificent pure white cliffs paraded before us. Peter was the musical director of *Praise Be*, the New Zealand version of *Songs of Praise*, which was taking place in Whitianga that weekend. He is in addition an internationally famous organist, as well as composer, conductor, accompanist, adjudicator, broadcaster and arts administrator. He has also been Concert Manager of the New Zealand Symphony Orchestra, Artistic Director of Wellington City Opera, and acting organist at Wellington Cathedral. He has been honoured for services to music. When Gerald mentioned the encounter to our musical cousin Richard in Wellington a few days later, it turned out, not entirely surprisingly, that he knew of Peter. Incidentally, by a 'small world' coincidence, a couple who boarded the boat with us, lived in a Scottish village where we had spent a holiday, so we had a quick response to their comment 'You won't know where we live in Scotland.'

Four cousins meet, New Zealand, 2006
L-R: Gerald, Angela, Richard, Rosemary

Going solo

During his last three decades, Gerald performed many solo roles. Some were with the great choirs with which he was associated—the English Concert Singers, directed by his great friend Roy Wales, in particular. He was also regularly singing solos in the choir at Wells Cathedral.

His first solo performances were in the mid-'80s. He wrote to Roy:

> I'm having a very exciting time singing.… I got some solos to sing for Goldsmiths Choral Union Summer Sing … so I did the necessary in the *Nelson Mass*, and this evening it's Kodaly's *Missa Brevis* and Britten's *Rejoice in the Lamb*. There aren't many notes to sing, but I think it's what is known as 'good experience'! If a fiver for expenses can be called a fee, these outings represent my professional debut!

Between these two events he had another solo experience:

> I went on a week's solo singing course at Charterhouse Summer School last week. There were about 50 on the course, and the tutors were Marion Studholme (who was so brisk as to be intimidating), Jean Allister, John Huw Davies and Duncan Robertson. Talk about jumping in at the deep end—after about 48 hours my head was spinning, and it was time to go home before I had time to put the whole tremendous experience into perspective. The highlights for me were two. First, a copy of *Sing Unto God* by Handel was thrust into my hand … and in foolhardy fashion I

undertook to sing the tenor solo.... It's all horrible semiquaver runs—
over 600 little black notes altogether. I know because I counted them out
of curiosity, and I found if I bashed at it in practice for more than about
20 minutes, I felt I was about to see as many again on the page. Anyway,
I duly sang this, backed by choir, orchestra, harpsichord, the lot, and only
went off the rails once, composing about three bars of Handel until I got
back in the slot. The upshot is I have a highly amusing tape of this *tour de
force*. Afterwards everybody was very kind, and couldn't understand how I
never seemed to take a breath.[1]

The other highlight happened like this. I cheekily joined those
auditioning for Verdi *Requiem* solos, this being the big piece in which all
the courses came together to round off the week. I admitted that I'd
never looked at it, as it just hadn't occurred to me that this could be me.
So I got the tenor in the *Lux Aeterna* trio, and on the day it felt fantastic;
unlike the impossible Handel, I got it all right, and sang with great power
when it was called for. (Personally, I blame all those Opera Gala Nights at
the Barbican.[2]) So I madly translate, whilst waiting for my next singing
job.[3]

I was chatting to one of my singing teachers in Doncaster, Kate
Lloyd-Evans, and told her this story. 'Oh,' she said, 'I was at the Summer
School at Charterhouse that year.' Not only that, she sang in the Verdi
Requiem with Gerald! She became a singer with Opera North and D'Oyly
Carte.

Subsequently there were many solo singing triumphs for Gerald. He
relished pitting himself against others and gaining feedback on his
performances. He pitched himself into music festivals in and near Wells,
and at least once at an eisteddfod. On that occasion, his Brahms rendition
was judged 'an excellent match of voice and song, musically secure and
with a good sense of style'. He wrote to a friend: 'I plucked up courage and
sang in one of the solo classes, and got quite a nice adjudication considering
I'd never entered a competition before. Obviously there were some aspects
which the judge gently pointed out as needing improvement too!' In 1989
the judge wrote 'Splendid choice for this sensitive singer … a great deal to
like here … a most attractive voice, well used'. This was for 'Whither Must
I Wander?' from *Songs of Travel* by Vaughan Williams. When it was
performed again at the Mid-Somerset Competitive Festival the following
year, the comments were: 'a fine voice, strong and even with excellent top'.

Gerald sang solos with the English Concert Singers, once as tenor soloist
in Handel's *Messiah* at Wells Cathedral when he was still in the choir there.
It was with the Hungarian Mendelssohn Chamber Orchestra, conducted by

---

[1] The recording still exists and, although it is of poor quality, Gerald's excellent voice and
the 600 semiquavers are there, followed by much applause.

[2] This refers to the London Chorale performances.

[3] He was buoyed up by his triumphs: the final sentence of this letter being handwritten.

Roy Wales. The review reported: 'All the soloists performed superbly', and Roy wrote to him 'Thank you very much for your lovely performance in *Messiah* … [and] for stepping in at short notice and doing such a good job.' (There were one or two occasions when he had been called on at short notice, not an easy task.) He repeated the performance at Lichfield Cathedral soon after, and in the following year at St Chad's Cathedral, Birmingham. In 1997 he was at Lewes Town Hall, and again Roy Wales wrote to him:

> Thank you for your fine contribution to the performance of the Beethoven *Choral Fantasia*. You will know from the reception how much the performance was appreciated, and for my part it was good to work with you and be involved in such an exhilarating end to the concert.

Gerald's voice was in demand locally, as he sang solos with choirs in such places as Yeovil, Glastonbury, Portishead, Wincanton, Clevedon and over the border at Tiverton in Devon. After a performance of Haydn's *Creation* with the Wincanton Choral Society, he received a letter: 'Many members of the audience commented on the quality of your singing…. You told the story with great conviction and expression, and you helped to bring the concert to life.' Praise indeed! In the Bath Minerva Choir he sang the part of Peter in both Handel's *The Passion of Christ* and Bach's *Cantata for Easter*.

Gerald's London friends claimed his time when he was living in Wells. He was the tenor soloist in Bach's *St John Passion* with South West London Choral Society, probably during a Wells choir holiday. With the Grove Singers in London he sang more Vaughan Williams, this time it was *Five Mystical Songs*, followed by Bruckner motets.

There were other concerts when he held the stage as a soloist. These were of the light music and song variety, and could be for raising money for a church or in a regular programme of concerts in the area. For example, the Strode Opera Company in Street staged concerts as well as operas. After one such *Music for You* evening, the newspaper reviewer wrote: 'Tenor, Gerald Burton set the atmosphere beautifully with a rounded and perfectly enunciated solo, and, indeed his entire contribution to the concert was immaculate.'

At a concert in Wells soon after his arrival in 1987, he sang all of Vaughan Williams's *Songs of Travel*. Friends wrote to him many years later, upon hearing that he was very ill: 'We remember with great affection your performance of *Songs of Travel*. It was wonderful.'

Two of Gerald's singing teachers

Gerald had many singing teachers in his various choirs. However, two teachers deserve special mention. While living in London, and singing frequently, Gerald decided it would be sensible to start having singing lessons. His London teacher was Richard Austin (1903–1989), son of singer-composer Frederick Austin. Richard had studied conducting at the Royal College of Music under Sir Adrian Boult and Sir Malcolm Sargent, and in Munich. He directed Carl Rosa Opera from 1929 to 1931, and succeeded Sir Dan Godfrey in charge of the Bournemouth Municipal Orchestra in 1934, resigning in 1940 when the war brought a reduction in the size of the orchestra. This later became the Bournemouth Symphony Orchestra.

After Gerald moved to Wells, his teacher was John Kentish (1910–2006), who had been a much-loved lyric tenor in British opera houses since joining Sadler's Wells Opera after war service. He delighted audiences at Glyndebourne, and appeared in 160 performances there between 1963 and 1977. He was said to have a perfect sense of comic timing. Later he became Director of the London Opera Centre, and Director of Opera at the Royal College of Music. He nurtured Kiri Te Kanawa at the London Opera Centre early in her career. During his long retirement in Wells, he was a founder member of the cathedral voluntary choir. He gave personal tuition to Gerald and other Vicars Choral at the cathedral. He and his wife saw Gerald on stage as Alfredo in *La Traviata*, a role John had played at Glyndebourne many years earlier.

'Through all the changing scenes'[1] ...

In the 1990s and into the next decade, Gerald entered the world of opera. At first he still had his commitments at Wells Cathedral, so he must have used his evenings and off-duty time to learn and rehearse the parts. When he visited us, he would often have a score with him.

The only operatic experiences that I recall when we were growing up were those of Uncle Henry, our mother's brother. We were taken to the Yorkshire coast at Withernsea and Bridlington to see him in Gilbert and Sullivan operettas and other musical theatre performances. Apart from these family outings, we visited the theatre when on holiday in Scarborough, and enjoyed variety shows like the *Fol-de-Rols*. We saw comedians such as Norman Evans with his *Over the Garden Wall* sketch, said to be the inspiration for the female characterisations by Les Dawson and Roy Barraclough many years later. We were taken to the Scarborough Open Air Theatre, wrapped in blankets, for the evening performances of such shows as *Hiawatha*, when the canoes were lit up and magically made their

---

[1] From the hymn: 'Through all the changing scenes of life', N. Tate and N. Brady, 1696.

way on the lake surrounding the stage. Other than playing parts in The
Company of the Way at St Mary's Church in Hull, and a brief experience of
acting when at university, I do not recall Gerald receiving any other stage
training.

When living in London he attended Sadler's Wells:

> The work was *Atalanta*, by Handel, written around 1730 and not
> performed for 150 years—and no wonder!... It had its amusing moments
> and the final scene was quite good.... It would have been quite pleasant
> music to go to sleep to, but the seats were too uncomfortable.

R: As Camille, Count de Rosillon, in *The Merry Widow* (Lehár)
Strode Opera, Street, 1990

I think that Gerald's voice was noticed in a concert near Wells, and he
was encouraged to join not one but several opera companies. A portfolio of
his performances showed seven appearances with three local companies.
His first performance was in 1990 as Camille de Rosillon in Lehar's *The
Merry Widow*. His knowledge of stagecraft was non-existent at the time, so
he must have been taught the various terms and techniques from scratch.
He told me that he had to learn names for the different parts of the stage
and the stage directions. In 1991 he played Hilarion in *Princess Ida* by
Gilbert and Sullivan. 1992 was a real triumph as he played Alfredo in *La
Traviata*. During his final illness, we were discussing his singing career with
a nurse; and Gerald told her that he had learned more than 90 pages of *La
Traviata*, and made only one mistake. I don't know the truth of this, but no
doubt he put in many hours of work to perfect his performance.

1993 saw Gerald as Pali, a young gipsy man in *The Gipsy Baron*, with music by Johann Strauss. He had to learn some dancing for this, as well as the acting. He subsequently appeared as Cyril in *Princess Ida*, and later in *The Grand Duke* (both by Gilbert and Sullivan) and the musical *Chess*.

As Ernest Dummkopf in *The Grand Duke* (Gilbert & Sullivan)
Wells Operatic Society, 2002

Brendan Sadler, Musical Director of Strode Opera wrote:

> It was my privilege to work with Gerald when he joined us for a number of shows and concerts, culminating in a production of Verdi's *La Traviata* in 1992 in which he took the role of Alfredo. His lyric tenor voice gave much pleasure to audiences and to other members of the company. His self-effacing manner, team spirit and his droll sense of humour earned him the respect and affection of all those who were fortunate enough to come into contact with him. He was one of that rare species today, a real gentleman.

A Parting Thought

For a parting thought, let us turn to Gerald, whose sense of humour we so enjoyed. The following is the final recorded example of it, spoken less than 48 hours before he died. One of his visitors casually mentioned that, on a journey back to Wells earlier that day, she had driven past Stonehenge. Gerald instantly replied:

'Yes, that's probably the best thing to do with it.'

2007